For Venus,
short star of
love and grace
♡ Jenn
813.618.4329

Creative Juice

Eight Weeks
to Authentic Writing

by Terra Pressler, Ph.D.

This book was published by Dancing Ink Press.
18835 Tracer Drive
Lutz, FL 33549

www.luvsounders.com

ISBN 0-9744997-0-6

Printed in the United States of America

Book design by Marty Megargee

Photos courtesy of Florida Citrus Growers

Library of Congress # 2001098946

Pressler, Terra

Creative Juice: Eight Weeks to Authentic Writing
by Terra Pressler/1st ed.

For my parents,
Paul and Lois Pressler

I want to thank:

My friend, Angie Jones,
for her excellent editing and unstinting support.

Charrie Moscardini, for her crackerjack copy-editing.

My students, who continually teach me,
and especially Clark Brook, Lucretia Austell,
Cher Tanner, and Marge Wesolowski,
for giving me permission to include their work in this book.

Wonderful film teacher, Claudia Johnson,
for allowing me to use her "Le Menu" exercise.

My sister, Carolyn Pressler, for her joyous encouragement
of everything I attempt, be it a triathlon or a book.

My parents, Lois and Paul Pressler,
for their generous support and ongoing inspiration.

Foremothers of the spiritual creativity movement,
Julia Cameron and Natalie Goldberg,
on whose shoulders I gratefully stand.

Marty Megargee for her top notch design services.

Florida Citrus Growers for their excellent photographs.
Drink more juice!

Nan Weed and Lyle Mayer
for their patience in producing dancing goddesses.

John Daugirda, Kate Lamson, Sylvia Foerstner, Kimen Mitchell, Fran Parker,
Marti Stevens Byers, Jim Lennon, Susan Taylor Lennon, Ellie Schwartz,
Barbara Sellers-Young, Diane Masiello, Debra Marrs, Bettie Perez,
Wolff Bowden, Liz Trupin-Pulli, and the many other friends and colleagues
who read, commented, and cheered-on this work.
You know who you are.

Contents

Beginnings

We are born juicy. Every one of us comes into the world dripping with creativity. Once upon a time, we all believed ourselves to be writers . . . and singers and painters and dancers. Ask the students in any kindergarten class if anyone is an artist and every hand flies up. Ask the same class in high school and you'll get only a few hands, tentatively raised. By full-blown adulthood, dust has settled where once bloomed a creative oasis and it's the rare duck who openly considers herself an "artist" or "writer."

Somewhere along the road to becoming, many of us seem to lose our most essential selves: our creative beings. Perhaps we've been conditioned out of thinking imaginatively. Maybe our creativity has been squashed by parents or teachers whose own spark was smothered, an inadvertent lineage of creative defeat. For lots of reasons, we tell ourselves we can't create. It's not practical. We lack talent. Who has time?

Yet the act of writing from our hearts is powerful, inexpressibly so. If you're reading this book, you value your creative source. At some level, you know writing can cleanse, fulfill, and lead you to your own authenticity. Writing is, at its best, joyful. At its very best, it is redemptive, both for the writer and the reader.

1

What will you get from a writing life? My students typically start this workshop wanting to improve their writing skills to get them ahead in careers or school or to gain approval and recognition. There's nothing wrong with that. Personally, I'd like to be on the bestseller list and make lots of money. But that's not why I write.

I write because it clears my head, engenders insight, leads me to my source, tickles me, coheres meaning. I write because writing produces work I'm proud of and because I can earn money doing something I love. I write because it gives me freedom. Physical freedom. Spiritual freedom.

Is writing always a bowl of literary cherries? Spare me. There are days I want to send my current manuscript through the shredder, draw and quarter it, and burn it at the stake. Then bury it in an unmarked grave. Rejection letters I'd just as soon not receive. Days when collecting for a freelance article takes longer than it took to write it.

But the truth is, a bad day writing is still better than a good day without it. Writing gives you the freedom to say whatever you want; as a twelve-year-old student put it, "You get to be more real than polite." Writing reveals your unique voice and at the same time connects you, establishes common ground with a reader. Individuation and universality on the same plate! Don't tell me writing isn't a feast.

There are a multitude of reasons to write. Think about what you want from writing, then imagine more and fill out this list.

Why Write?

1. _It helps earn me some cash,_
2. _Time goes by in a flash._
3. _I want to produce another book_
4. _It helps me research a new outlook_
5. _People enjoy my spin on what's been said_
6. _Writing is how I sort the thoughts in my head_

You want to write. That's established. So how do you go about it?

Writers write, axiomatic as it is true. Yes, they also sit at a desk, sharpen pencils, stare out the window, boot up, shake down, fall out, look within. Sooner or later, though, the words have to go down on paper. This book is about how to make that happen. We'll start with a couple of basic habits to cultivate that will lead you into writing every day.

Free Writing

Censor-free writing is a great tool to get your writing moving. Julia Cameron, author of *The Artist's Way,* the book which sparked the current "spiritual creativity" movement, urges readers to write "morning pages," which she defines as three pages of uncensored, speedy writing the first thing every morning. Dr. Susan Perry, a social psychologist who studies creativity, recommends spending fifteen minutes every day letting the words come out on their own, what she calls "writing in flow." Natalie Goldberg, Zen mother of spiritual journaling and author of *Writing Down the Bones*, likewise encourages writers to avoid judging their own work, to throw down the words as they come from the deepest places.

Regardless of the method, this type of journal keeping is guaranteed to produce a surge in your creativity. Whatever you discover works for your process is what you should do—pen or keyboard, morning or evening, three pages or fifteen minutes. But for now, two things are non-negotiable. Do the journaling regularly and do it fast, without censoring. Put your pencil to paper or your fingers to keyboard and don't lift again until time's up. Let it all out and I mean *all*.

This is important. Mama don't allow no self-censorship around here. Let everything spill onto the page in a big gush. Will you get junk? Yes, and that's the good news. If you get it onto the page, there's a much better chance it won't be clogging up your mind when you go to create.

Mornings are good because you haven't filled your cranium with extraneous stuff yet and it's more likely "pure you" will come out. But if mornings don't work, journal when you can. Regularly. Every day is your goal. This isn't your serious writing, although you'll get plenty of great ideas from the activity. This is your warm-up. No athlete would think of charging into her sport without warming up. Why should a creative athlete? Will you fall off the wagon? On a consistent basis. Get back on—especially if you're feeling dry or trying to work out a thorny issue. Eventually, you'll get to where you're writing everyday anyway and this won't be as important, but it's still a great tool for every level of writer.

There's one more non-negotiable point. This journal is for your eyes only. You have to be able to write *anything*, plenty of which you may not want loved ones to see. It may not devastate your neighbor to learn her way of handling stress through incessant talking drives you crazy, but it may not be something you're ready to tell her. If you have to buy a lock box because of prying eyes, do it. Hide your writing, if necessary, but make it safe to say anything at all.

Keeping this journal will accomplish several things critical to a creative artist. It will clean the page for serious work by washing out all the junk. It will tone your writing muscles. And it will birth brilliant ideas you can capitalize on in your work. As a side-benefit, you'll save thousands of dollars in therapy bills. I say it lightly, but in truth, free writing helps you explore your farthest reaches and that may be the greatest benefit of all.

These pages may be completely uninfluenced—whatever comes out in the moment—or they may come out in response to a specific prompt. At least one day during this week's journaling, mull this: what obstacles have I thrown in the way of my creativity? Simply put those words at the top of the page, then zoom. As usual, write as fast as you can without censoring anything.

You may find, when you first start, you're getting a lot of resistance, skepticism . . . the usual self-sabotage flak. Take heart. If all you can write is "I have nothing to say. This is so bogus. Blah blah blah and yadda yadda yadda," so be it. Keep writing. Once you get thoroughly fed up with "blah blah blah," your creative self will kick in. After about two pages of the "blahs," you'll experience a breakthrough. Trust it. Write.

If you're making yourself crazy, use this prompt: "What I really want to say is . . ." Then see what comes out. You may also use "What I really need to say is . . ." Use whichever works best for you. The main thing is that you do it. Make every day your goal. Don't beat yourself up if you get bucked off the untamed pen, but do saddle up and get back on.

Make Spontaneous Writing Easy

Always carry a small notebook with you. Use it to jot down ideas, interesting snatches of conversation, significant images and whatever else your creative juice notices. Make your notebook small enough to travel with you, but not so small it's ineffective. I like the old-fashioned composition notebooks, which fit handily into my over-sized purse. An unused date book works nicely, as well, and will fit in a fanny pack on a hike. Lately, small, fat, spiral notebooks have become available, a perfect fit in a cargo pocket.

Keep paper and pencil beside your bed. You will never, ever remember that brilliant idea or turn of phrase you were certain was branded on your brain so you didn't write it down. Write it down, even in the middle of the night.

Start with "I Am"

Is there anything in the world more interesting to us than ourselves? Nope. Regardless how green or how stuck you are, you can always write an "I am" poem, a free-for-all, beginning with the words "I am . . ." The word "poem" can be a big word. Not in this case. This doesn't have to rhyme or even make sense. You're playing with words like babies play with blocks.

In Susan Wooldridge's wonderful book, _Poemcrazy_, she talks about "I am" poems. She suggests you write down words on cheap carnival tickets available in an art or educational supply store. Find words from field guides, weather books, anything to give you ideas for a "word pool." You can dip into this pool anytime you're stuck. Just reach in a hand and pull out a fistful of words.

I am the ORIGINAL CHOCOLATE COVERED NUT.
A Genuine ... Classic. Since 1974

I prefer to write lists of at least twenty adjectives, fifteen nouns and fifteen verbs, then mix and match. You can do this through free association or use the following prompts.

Get Juicy

This exercise generates a pool of words to dive into, particularly helpful when starting out or if you're feeling dry. Don't think too hard about these. Just throw them down as they come.

Adjectives: Write three adjectives (<u>w</u>ords <u>that</u> <u>describe</u>) that come to mind when you think about the following words:

nun

polite , pure abstinence , prayerful

square dancing

cute do ce doe , circular partner , country

summer day

Bright , humid , Steamy

dolphin

wet , Smart , smooth

home

happy , heavenly , Secure

Leonardo da Vinci

genius , gifted , defiant

tropical storm

electrical , _raging_ , _brewing_

cat

Sneaky , _quick_ , _independent_

Nouns: List two pairs of opposite things; for example, day and night, bare feet and shoes:

love and _fear_

Joy and _pain_

List two pairs of related but disparate things, like horns and strings, peanut butter and jelly:

laces and _Sneakers_

Pillow and _head_

List three natural things, like river, mountain, wind:

tree , _bird_ , _grass_

List three flighty, silly things, like crinoline, jingle bell, or butterfly:

Bow ties , _Barretts_ , _Bingo_

List three grand things, like canyon, miracle, sky:

rainbow , _Sun_ , _thunderbolt_

I am electrical laces tying up sneaky grass under Sneakers. I am independent love rounding up Bowties & Barretts for Bandaging of Birds. I am measuring Joy and pain. and writing quick.

Verbs: write at least three active verbs that relate to each of the following professions: *ing*

nurse

preps (ing) , Bandages , writes

musician

plays piano, dances , nods on beat

scientist

pokes , examines , performs

ranch hand

ROUNDS UP , yodles , labors

carpenter

hammers , sweeps , measures

When you finish your list, review it. If you don't like any of the words, cross them out and put in some you do. Now, using your list and any other words you want, write an "I am" poem. For example, "I am a bald mountain dancing in feathers. I am blue and rich and wild for canyons." It may make no rational sense. Trust it. It will make intuitive, lyrical sense. Keep going. Once you're flowing, you may want to ditch the list and use words that stream from your pen.

Remember, it doesn't have to make sense. My student, Cher Tanner wrote: "I am a glowing, performing shooting star. Frisky and fun, pirouetting my bountiful way through torrents steamy. Hot fudge sundaes." Works for me.

Get Juicy

Another way to generate a pile of words is with this computer menu-inspired exercise. Take an evocative image or piece of music that draws you. Study it, listen to it. Then fill out the maze on page 14. List an adjective the image or music inspires. Maybe you've chosen a pristine mountain scene. Studying it, let's say the adjective that comes to mind is "majestic." From that adjective, associate two nouns. For each of those nouns, associate two verbs. For each of those verbs, associate two more adjectives. Don't concern yourself with being clever. The words may inspire you to ask, "What's the plural of banal?" but don't worry about it; you'll put them together in creative ways. Each completed map will entail fourteen words and will look something like this filled-in pattern, based on the hypothetical mountain scene.

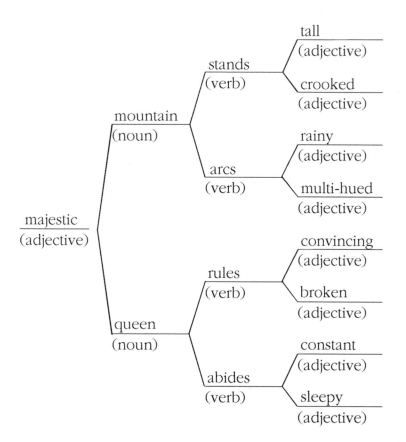

My other words from this image were:

- crisp
- air
- breathes
- pure
- innocent
- floats
- light
- blue
- cracker
- cowcatches (it's a Southern thang)
- spindly
- bovine
- salts
- earthy
- metallic

Together with the earlier map, I had plenty of words.

The next step is to throw out any words you don't like and substitute words you do. I didn't want "bovine" or "metallic," so I substituted "ruminative" and "glinting."

Note for you English teachers and other grammarians: if it drives you nuts to write an adjective after a verb, go ahead and write the adverb, then convert it to an adjective. For example, "sleepily" becomes "sleepy." Adverbs don't have nearly the punch of adjectives and, generally, you're better off without them. A cardinal rule in writing is "Show, don't tell." Rather than, "Angie put down the phone angrily," consider "Angie slammed down the phone." Says it without the adverb. Shows rather than tells.

Of course all rules, including this one, are meant to be broken; but think about the strongest writing you've encountered. Chances are it contains far more adjectives than adverbs and far more nouns and verbs than adjectives. Even adjectives should be used sparingly except in poetic writing. Show, don't tell.

Once you have your list of words, mix and match. For example, "The strong queen breathes salt air." Now, adapt to an "I am." "I am a salt queen, pure and strong. Abiding and true." Hey, it doesn't have to be on the list! Throw down words and play. This is practice; there are no critics kibitzing over your shoulder.

Fill in your own blanks on the next page.

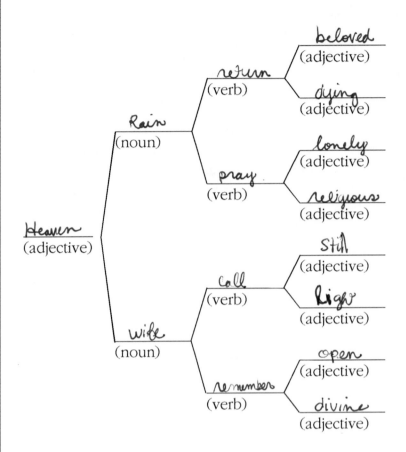

Once you've completed this pattern, do it again, with the same image or a different one. The same piece of music or another. This will give you sufficient words to play the "I am" game. Use the words to recognize your deepest self. Sing it, shout it, dance it. Celebrate the song of yourself. "I am a footfall of God. A cobalt streak in a pure white sky." Or this from my student, Marge Wesolowski: "I am a pastoral hillside on which houses flow in soft, slow ascent to the sky."

Substituting the Great Excuses with Balance and Wisdom

We have perfectly reasonable excuses why we aren't as creative as we'd like to be. And that's just what they are: excuses. It's time we pack up our cherished reasons for being less than we are and send them screaming out the door like a bad Edvard Munch imitation. (Remember the painting of the anguished little man with the big, screaming head on the bridge?)

During this process, you'll contact your inner voice, that deep wisdom which informs a creative life. Everything you need to know is already within you, but it may be buried under years of "shoulds" or decades of "can'ts." Explore your own shoulds and can'ts and how they obstruct your writing.

Sit quietly. Drop deep. Allow all the pernicious excuses to bubble up. Why didn't you write yesterday? Why not today? List all the reasons you haven't become the creative artist you want to be. Sing the "Why I can't write" blues. Here are a few I regularly flirt with: I'm too old. I'm too busy. I have too many other responsibilities. I'm not good enough. I'm too fat (huh?). If I haven't by now, it's not going to happen (a variation on the "too old" theme). I don't have anything to say. It's too competitive.

Your actual highway mileage may vary—maybe you consider yourself too young, too good for corrupt commercial success, too lacking in imagination, too tired, too scared. Whatever your reasons, put them down. Literally. Lay them down on the page. At the end of this workshop, or anytime before, if you're ready to release all the excuses, to lay them down for good, tear up the page and consign it to flame in a small but meaningful ritual of your own making.

What are the top reasons you can't write? If you're a mother, the answer is easy. Who has time? If you're sensitive, it'll be easy, too. What makes you think you're good enough? What are your reasons?

Get Juicy

Reasons I Can't Write. . .

1. Need a community of support *(meeting with AD in westchase)) collab labs*
2. Need the discipline of a classroom *(checking in with Terra)*
3. Don't know what's most important *(I'm doing God's will)*
4. Need approval of subjects and lack Direction *(invest career coach)*
5. Time management Skills suck / Waste of Time
6. Not going to Promote it anyway *(project mgmt (seek out marketing /promotions majors))*
7. Don't want to Tour or Perform often *(invest time in video sketches + Blog)*
8. Not talented enough *(create an affirmation to address this)* Answer Screen call engineer

Popular excuses my students typically list: *memorize moms*

1. Not enough time.
2. Too many obligations and responsibilities.
3. Can't concentrate.
4. Lack direction, don't know what to write. Nothing to say.
5. Not talented enough.
6. Lack of a supportive environment.

7. Fear of failure.

8. Fear of success.

9. Fear of overshadowing a parent.

10. Fear of "going there" and meeting my shadow. Fear of the honesty it would require of me.

11. Fear I'll get into it, but won't complete anything, then have that on my conscience.

12. Self-censorship, over-control of what words I can put down (a literary variant of common, everyday perfectionism).

13. Lack of discipline.

Boiled down, these reasons not to write tend to fall into two camps: time and self-esteem obstructions. Let's look at both.

Time

We have as much time as we have. Yeah, that sounds like Alfred E. Newman's take on a Zen koan, but consider it. Busy Americans have enough time to watch TV a whopping three and a half hours a day, on average, all of which could be spent creating. We have time to read the paper and drink that second cup of coffee. Who needs the aggravation of more bad news? Take that half hour and write a poem. We have time to spend an average of one and a half hours preparing a meal. One word: "take-out."

Get Juicy

Track an average day. Carry around a small notebook—it can be the one I suggested you carry as a matter of course for ideas. Find out for yourself just how much open time you actually have.

I suspect you'll find time you never knew was there. Include periods where you have to be somewhere but are really on hold. Hanging out waiting for your son to finish soccer practice, waiting for a client; I've been known to jot at long red lights. Take out your notebook. Sketch out a scene. Write imagined character studies of people around you—they may show up in a novel someday. Describe your immediate environment. Make sure to use every sense, including the so-called sixth sense, which synthesizes the other five and produces intuition.

Today, at the assisted living facility where I volunteer, I met a sweet couple who had been married for seventy-two years. Florence and Willard held hands during the garden club, as unselfconscious as plants. One ninety-one-year-old with a virtually unlined face told me sweetly, "My name is Lavinia. I'm from Virginia. I used to be an avid gardener, you know." The woman was a walking poem. Don't let these simple miracles go uncharted. Write them. You have the time.

Kids, especially small kids, present a special challenge for finding time. Children grow up in a breath, but those five years or so of indentured servitude feel like forever. Getting them in school will change everything. The world will open like a gardenia blossom. Until then, negotiate. Consider day care for at least part of the day. Absolutely commit to taking time for yourself whenever they're napping.

I have a fundamental rule that made a friend wide-eyed when I told her about it: If the house is quiet, with just me in it, I absolutely may not do anything domestic. It's my time to create. That may mean taking a long bath or reading a book. Usually it means writing. All that domestic goddess stuff can be done when the brood's in the nest, with the added pay-off it will at least stand a chance of being noticed and receive a sconce of credit. Okay, that was a little joke to leaven the atmosphere. But seriously, don't putter when you could be creating, unless that's part of your process. Joyce Carol Oates gets ideas as she vacuums— whatever moves your pen.

Simultaneous full-time work *and* parenting present an even greater challenge. Do whatever you can—swap with other parents, participate in a baby-sitting co-op, hire a neighbor kid to take your kids to the park. Whatever it takes, buy yourself regular creating time. Get up twenty minutes earlier. Let the kids do more for themselves—do you really have to pack all the lunches? If you have a caring partner, talk with him or her to get parity or at least more help. You may have to discuss it a few thousand times. Keep at it.

I'm not saying it's easy, but I am saying it can be done. I wrote and performed a one-woman show when my son was two. Was it easy? No. Did it save my creativity and thus my sanity? Absolutely.

You notice I equate creativity and sanity. Yep. For those of us who need to create, who were born with an inherent drive to express ourselves creatively, the act of creation does indeed become salvation, sanity, and fulfillment. Without it we get edgy and neurotic and obsessive. The old myth that artists are crazy myths by a mile. Artists are crazy only if they're not allowed to create. Here's the sad part. We're all artists. Some of us just remember it.

Set priorities. Where does your creative life land on the list? Cherish yourself and your creativity enough to fight for it.

Get Juicy

Draw a balloon bouquet of your life. Eight balloons will represent areas of your life. Inflate these balloons to various degrees of fullness, depending on how fully realized that area of your life is. The areas I'd like you to consider are:

- Creativity
- Work/Career
- Home
- Family/Primary Relationships

- Spirituality
- Adventure/Leisure
- Friendships/Social life
- Health

So, let's say your family life is terrific—loving spouse, great kids. That balloon would be fully inflated. But say your spiritual life is on the skids. Spiritual life? What spiritual life? That balloon would be a limp little trouper, the one you find behind the couch weeks after the party. Maybe your career is so-so. That balloon would be half-inflated. Is your home a comfortable palace that suits you down to the ground, or a disorganized hovel? More likely it falls somewhere in the great middle; inflate accordingly. Once you're finished, you'll have a graphic image of your life.

Mind you, I don't want to impose my values on you. Let's say your spiritual balloon is flat as a pancake, but you're a devout atheist and that's fine by you. Or your home is listed in the annals of "Early American Depression Decorating," and was the keystone entry in "Twenty Fanciful Ways to Put a Car up on Blocks," but you've chosen it as your version of voluntary simplicity. You decide the priorities in your life.

Now list them, in order, based on how much you value each. Ascribe particular activities to each item. For example, under "friends and family," perhaps you'll list "spending quality time with friends and family;" under "health," perhaps "exercise" or "eight hours sleep every night." If "spirituality" is on your list, describe what that means to you, whether it's church, meditation, or walks in the forest. Creativity might include making music, writing, painting, dancing, or floating down a river. You've got to fill the well, after all.

When you've finished, go back and note the average amount of time per week you currently spend on each priority.

Get Juicy

Priorities

1. _Home_

and that means _Sorting_ time spent _____

and that means _cooking_ time spent _____

and that means _cleaning_ time spent _____

2. _Family_

and that means _phone conversations_ time spent _____

and that means _dining together_ time spent _____

and that means _playing a game_ time spent _____
(Soul parade)
(uno)

3. _Friendships_

and that means _phone conversations_ time spent _____

and that means _Facebook Comments_ time spent _____

and that means _respond to computer_ time spent _____
notches

4. _____ Spirituality _____

and that means __gratitude journal__ time spent _____

and that means __meditation__ time spent _____

and that means __prayer__ time spent _____

5. _____ Health _____

and that means __Gilad__ time spent _____

and that means __finding good recipes__ time spent _____

and that means __planning vacation__ time spent _____

6. _____ Work/Career _____

and that means __memorizing work__ time spent _____

and that means __mailing contacts__ re: publish or Booking time spent _____

and that means __Promoting with Blog/Flyer__ time spent _____

7. _____ Creativity _____

and that means __morning pages__ time spent _____

and that means __supporting art collabs__ strengthen piano/Drum/voice/paint time spent _____

and that means __More character development__ time spent _____

8. _____ Adventure/Leisure _____

and that means __relaxing in hammock__ time spent _____

and that means __reading/research__ time spent _____

and that means __listening to music__ New: time spent _____

If you're spending little time on a top-rated priority, but massive amounts on one that's near the bottom or not on the list at all, you need to ask yourself why. If you're giving your creativity short shrift, especially ask why.

Often, an unfulfilling job looms large in this exercise. With family responsibilities and an uncertain workplace, the idea of changing careers, much less jobs, can be daunting and may be unnecessary. Maybe the job you have can be tweaked to become more fulfilling and creative. Consider lateral moves you can make or changes in the work environment that would move your job up the list of what you value. If not and it's abrading your spirit on a daily basis without at least giving life lessons—some of the most infuriating people I've ever met have been my most valuable teachers—consider change.

I left a successful law career to go into theater. Most rational people would consider this something less than the best career move in the world. Okay, most rational people would consider it nuts. But I was waking up every morning groaning about another day in court and every night delighting in being on stage at the local theater. A radical shift was right for me. And I had a supportive partner and no kids. I'm not saying it's easy. Don't leap without psychological and occupational preparation. Take what schooling you need, save up for the transition, prep the family. Then, do what you need to do.

Self-Esteem Obstructions

These include "I'm not good enough" and variants like "I have nothing to say," "I'm dry," "I've never been very creative."

Here's what's true. When you peel back these reasons layer by layer like a rotted onion, at the core, down in that swampy unconscious, lies fear. I'm too scared. Scared of failure. Scared of success. Both have their price. But repressing your creativity has an even greater price.

Creative folk often fear they'll discover they're bona fide nuts if they break off those cozy chains of busy-busy and gotta-gotta and let the naked self out for lunch. One student said she doesn't fulfill herself creatively because she's "afraid of going there," afraid of dropping down to the wettest, darkest places. What's true is that the tremendous energy expended in denial and suppression is ultimately far more wearing and painful than confronting your personal demons. I'm a recovering alcoholic; trust me on this. Trust that becoming more fully creative means becoming more fully alive. You go sane, not insane.

What's important here is to distinguish between creativity and socially determined "success." Look deep. Mull in your journal. How much do you confuse these two very different things? If you consider your creativity to be valid only if someone is paying you big bucks, you've set yourself up. That isn't to say you don't deserve to be paid big bucks. You do. But create for yourself. Is writing only good if it's published? Is that what's holding you back? That your work—and, says the tangled psychic machinery, therefore you—might not be accepted?

Here's the riddle. The only way you'll ever produce work worthy of public acclaim is by acting as if the public doesn't exist. Produce work worthy of your own acclaim. The rest will follow. We create because it's what we do, who we are. A bad day writing is better than a good day not writing.

Ask yourself if you want to create strictly to gain others' admiration. That's not a bad thing, but it's important to know. If so, you'll want to skew your work toward what's currently fashionable. When I was a baby actor, and well beyond if I'm honest, I got a tremendous thrill from applause, lived for it. Standing ovations sent me over the moon. Then a strange thing happened. Slight, fluffy acting jobs became only work, despite how much applause they garnered. I only enjoyed the process if the play was meaningful, the cast worth being around. Finally, I only wanted to be on stage if there was a deep spiritual connection between the audience and me, if the acting was a form of prayer. I had been participating in an art to feed an immature ego. That beats shooting off a few rounds from a book tower or drinking yourself to death, but it lacked the depth of meaning, connection and pure joy that creation can provide.

I'm not saying creation is only valid if it's solely for yourself. After all, any art is by its nature a form of communication. But I am saying it's good to know why we do what we do; if we're creating in a medium or genre because it gets us strokes and we're really not happy doing it, we've missed the point. Creating makes us happy—happier than we can imagine. We go swing dancing with imagination and we don't ever want to stop. Creating gives us juice, energy, vivid life. Would you create even if you never saw a word in print. . . the inside of a gallery. . . your scenes on a screen? I hope so. It makes you happier to create. You wouldn't be reading this book if it didn't.

Does that mean you should create in a vacuum and not worry about filthy lucre? Of course not. You deserve to get paid for your work and paid well. Our culture devalues art enough; its producers certainly shouldn't. But retain the wall between financial and artistic success. Don't confuse the two. Critics and agents and editors and the consuming public determine financial success. You and only you determine artistic success. If there is one thing in this life that is yours and yours alone, it is your creativity.

Creativity is inextricably linked with authenticity. When you're down deep, being true to yourself, you are at your most imaginative. Everything else falls away.

Fran, a member of my writing group, Write Women, tells me my work has deepened significantly since I became chronically ill several years ago. I'm well now, but for five years I had my belly to the universe in physical surrender. The spiritual deepening was forced and pronounced. For the first time in my life I had nothing but the bare self, devoid of credentials and other props. When you're flat on the floor, what do you have but your authentic self? From that supine position, I learned a lot about myself and what's important to me. I learned priorities.

Here's one priority I discovered, perhaps the biggest one: Speak your truth. If creative expression had to be reduced to a single aphorism it would be this. Speak your truth. Anything else is entertainment. There's nothing wrong with that, but it's a different species, mineral to vegetable. Your truth will vary and evolve and shape-shift on a daily basis. It may generate raucous laughter or lyric tears, but it will hold the only hallmark worth having—your own truth.

Don't confuse this with selfishness. I've facilitated several Artist's Way groups and found a tendency in some participants to use this maxim as an excuse to welch on commitments or even turn downright ugly. Truth isn't always pretty, but if it's authentic, it is invariably expressed in love. Rough, tough, angry, perhaps, but with love in the ultimate sense of that word, the sense that knows beyond reckoning that we are separate from each other only through carefully maintained illusion. We're swapping atoms right now, you and I; what a great thing. Sit some day across from some one and breathe in as the other breathes out, breathe out as the other breathes in, back and forth like a two-person saw of silk shearing the air. Hard to know who's breathing whom after awhile.

Jumping the Obstacles

In this exercise, you're going to tackle your "Reasons I Can't Write," one by one, with a specific game plan and affirmation. If your issue is time, scratch down your commitment to keep track of an average day so you can find undiscovered pockets of free time. List specific plans and goals with a timeline for when you intend to accomplish them. Finally, add an affirmation, a commitment to yourself and your creative life. For example:

Previous excuse *No Time*

Game Plan   *Talk to Betty next door about childcare swap by the end of this week. Buy pocket notebook to use during coffee breaks and do time exercise*

Affirmation   *I have enough time to be a wildly creative writer.*

Integrate these affirmations by gently repeating them to yourself during periods when you're deeply relaxed and receptive, such as just before you fall asleep and upon waking, during meditation, or deep relaxation.

Also, somewhere in this exercise, consider the affirmation "I devote at least one hour a day to my creative life." Think about it: if you wrote just one page a day, by the end of one year, you'd have 365 pages of a first draft. The year's going to pass anyway. Don't let it pass you by. Create something along the way.

If your issue is lack of confidence, you'll need to dig deeper. First you have to discover what fears lurk beneath the lack of confidence. Did you have a parent who consistently modeled the impossibility of being a creative artist? Julia Cameron talks about "shadow artists," those people who would have loved to fulfill themselves creatively but, because of their own fears, held back—became an English teacher instead of a writer, a docent rather than an artist. Often, they project their own unconscious grief at this loss of their artistic self onto others, discouraging a creative life because they were denied one.

Did you have a beloved teacher give you a "D" in art in fifth grade? I did and I didn't touch anything remotely resembling the visual arts until I got into graduate school and another beloved teacher broke apart the fallacy I had no abilities in that area. With his encouragement, I've enjoyed playing in an array of arts and crafts since. Am I very good? Nah. But I enjoy it and am at least good enough to have sold a few masks.

Don't wait for a mentor to heal you from a childhood setback. Let yourself recall those people who hurt your creative self, bring the wounds out to the light of day and let them heal. Get good and angry with those who sought to trample your creativity, then forgive them. If you need to clear out creative squelchers from your past who continue to cramp your present, here's one way to do it.

Get Juicy

This exercise came to me during a long hike. It involves what is essentially walking meditation. If that sounds too wooey-wooey for you, I also offer an adapted "Alternative Juice" exercise at the end. Do I believe in contemplative practice? More than I can say. I strongly encourage you to give the creative visualization and deep relaxation practices in this book a try. But I also understand you may feel resistance, so I have alternatives included. Do what is comfortable for you—and then a little more.

Some background is in order: several months before I hit on this exercise, a teaching assistant at the university where I taught had busted my chops big time, for no apparent reason. I'd had only glowing reviews as a teacher until then and was devastated. And mad. And having trouble letting go. This was back in the days before I understood that criticism says more about the criticizer than the criticized. For me, resentment is toxic; it gets me stuck in every way, including creatively. I needed release. Here's how I found it.

Plan a long walk in nature, somewhere beautiful and inspiring. If that's not an option, do this at home; but in either case, give yourself plenty of time and guaranteed solitude. The cast of characters you'll be inviting in includes everyone who has shamed, belittled or otherwise put down your creative self. You can mull these beforehand in your journal, or trust they'll show up when you're ready.

Walk with gentle, reverent steps. The great spiritual leader, Thich Nhat Hanh, suggests you "kiss the earth" with every footfall. Notice your surroundings with acuteness and gratitude. Without those trees, you'd have no breath, without the sun, no light. Feel the color of the sky. Smell the green of the leaves. Let every sense soar and commingle with every other. It may take some time to shuck off the anxieties of the day, but if you give yourself over to noticing the earth, it will happen.

Then, begin to notice your breath. Don't seek to change it, simply notice it. Notice how many steps you take on the in-breath, how many on the out. Continue this count for several minutes. Then, count your in- and out-breaths up to ten, returning to one if you lose track. In and out for one, in and out for two . . . this breath-work will aid in heightening your senses. Keep at it until you notice a greater lucidity, a calm that floats in your center and radiates out. This will likely happen after about twenty minutes. Give it a chance.

When you feel this calm center, think back on the people you hold resentment toward, those who have wronged your creative being. One by one, call up the face of the person who has hurt you. Review what the person did to you. Let yourself feel fully the grief and hurt.

If you're like me, feeling anger is often problematic. Lots of us weren't allowed to express anger in our childhood homes, resulting in vast reservoirs of suppressed emotion. But in this exercise you're alone and safe. Let your feelings course through you as long as they need to in order to be fully expressed.

Caveat: re-experiencing anger often breeds more anger. That's not the point here. Anger is typically a mask for need. Look behind and below the rage at what was really going on for you. Maybe the person's behavior invoked shame in you, or self-doubt, or intimidation. If you find yourself awash in ever-increasing waves of rage with nowhere to go with it, move on to the next step. Ideally, though, you'll experience your emotions fully and feel yourself come full circle, back to a place of repose.

When your emotional charge is spent and the heat cools, gently—as gently as you would cradle a newborn—imagine yourself into the person who wronged you. How was it for them? Why did they feel the compulsion to do what they did? Maybe it was completely one-sided, but more likely there were ways you planted seeds for the experience.

Looking deeply, I had to admit I hadn't been sensitive to my teaching assistant's needs. She had initially put me on a pedestal, then over several weeks had become increasingly flaky about course responsibilities. I'd shrugged my shoulders and finally become irritated, rather than asking what was going on. My neglect had planted seeds. Had I deserved to be flamed so drastically? Of course not. But, for a while I could feel how it must have been for her: someone from whom she needed emotional attention had progressively ignored her. I understood her motivation.

I took the lesson from this experience, then spent a good long while releasing her, forgiving her. I did this by placing her in my heart and saying to myself with as much love as I could muster, "I forgive you." I paid attention to the emotional response with every "I forgive you." Sometimes I fell into forgiveness like a kid into chocolate pudding. Other times I felt resistance; "I forgive you" sounded a lot like "Screw you." Self-righteousness. Cold indifference. I kept repeating "I forgive you" until I felt no emotional charge at all for several repetitions.

Then, it was time to move on to forgiving myself. I surprised myself with that part, but looking back, it makes perfect sense. Don't skip this step. Forgive yourself completely. It's the only way to be whole and well.

Repeat this process with as many creative enemies as needed. Remember, you're forgiving these people for yourself, not for them. By doing so, you in no way condone their activities or tacitly give permission to be dumped on in the future. This is for you. Forgive as much and as many as you can; repeat as necessary until you feel truly cleansed. Then move on.

Alternative Juice

Pull out your trusty notebook in a safe, quiet space. Clear your head. Stare at a dust mote, listen to calming music, do whatever you do to ease yourself into a receptive frame of mind.

Write across the top of a page: "People who squashed my creativity." Initially, make a brief list, e.g., Mom, when she said my Madonna poem was too "out there"; Miss Mallory, when she gave me a "D" in art; Dad, when he didn't like my short story. Add to it. Write the specific scenes in detail. Who was there? What were they wearing? How did they sound? Write out the dialogue, if there was any. How you felt. I can still remember getting back my painting with the big, red "D" across the top, and the initial shock of disbelief followed by floods of shame. I had used crazy colors—lime green for the sky, orange for skin. I thought it was cool. Miss Mallory did not.

Once you've written out the scene and your emotions, write "I forgive you," then write the immediate reaction, whether it's "Sure I do" or "horse pucky," or "blank." Once you've reached no emotional charge whatsoever for several entries, you're ready to move on to writing from your former enemy's perspective.

Miss Mallory was an older, African-American woman teaching in a predominantly white school in the '50s. She had probably learned young and well: *If you want to survive and get ahead, don't rock the boat*. Lime green skies could swamp you. Perhaps in her mind, she committed an act of love, a hard lesson toward a better life. Small town Indiana isn't keen on nonconformists. Had I stayed there, lime green skies would have defined and constrained me.

Once you feel you've gleaned what insights you need and forgiven creative squelchers, you're ready to fill out your game plan.

Get Juicy
Reasons I Can Write . . .

Flip back to page 16 where you list the reasons you can't write.
Now convert them to reasons why you can.

writers conference

Gather these specific poets

what time ae will meet they Sat 9-3pm monthly

1. Previous excuse _Need a community of support_

   Game Plan _*I will seek out talented writers I admire for counsel and I will find joy through fellowship_

   Affirmation _I am supporting and being supported by a great group of artists + writers._

2. Previous excuse _Need the discipline of a classroom_

   Game Plan _* I_ _____

   _____

   _____

   _____

   Affirmation _____

   _____

3. Previous excuse _____

   Game Plan _____

   _____

   _____

   _____

terrapressler @ comcast.net

Due on

33

Affirmation   _____

_____

4. Previous excuse   _____

Game Plan   _____

_____

_____

Affirmation   _____

_____

5. Previous excuse   _____

Game Plan   _____

_____

_____

Affirmation   _____

_____

6. Previous excuse   _____

Game Plan   _____

_____

_____

Affirmation   _____

_____

7. Previous excuse _____

   Game Plan   _____

                    _____

                    _____

   Affirmation   _____

                    _____

8. Previous excuse _____

   Game Plan   _____

                    _____

                    _____

   Affirmation   _____

                    _____

As you work through this book, you'll discover more tools and insights. After completing each week's chapter, swing back to this section and add to it.

Tools and Insights

Developing Sensate Awareness: Simple Miracles

If there is any single maxim for fulfilling yourself creatively, it's this: *Pay attention.* Want the graduate course? *Pay careful attention.* Whole-body creativity is what you're after, nothing less. I want you to dance with your mouth, sing with your hands, taste the earth in all its glory.

Simple Miracles

Attend to simple miracles. You have five of them, six if you count synthesis of all the senses—incarnate intuition. The senses are a writer's best friends, the creative spirit's very fuel.

The Simple Miracle of Sight

There may be none so blind as those who will not see, but there are also none so acute as those who will. Open your eyes. Look deeply. This is easy to say, but tough to do. Babies have it naturally, but for adults who've spent a lifetime unlearning native curiosity, awareness takes discipline and training.

Get Juicy

In every drive of even the shortest duration, look for at least one simple visual miracle. If you look closely, it will be there, but you have to be open to see it. When I visit my friend Marti, I drive a country road to her house. One summer day I rounded a curve and there, backlit in the late-afternoon sun, was a fantastic, shining figure from the future. The radiant being glinted silver and had long, geometric wings. As I drew closer, the figure became a slouching farm kid holding a TV antenna. Simple miracle.

The next day, along the same road, I saw a calf gambol with a red plastic bag. It literally leapt straight up for several feet in exuberant bliss as the red bag gusted from breeze to breeze. Simple miracle.

This morning, on the prototypically prosaic drive from the grocery store to my house, I waited at a red light, fretting because I hadn't found my simple miracle and was almost home. Then, in the berm, I noticed two newly planted saplings. Both had a few blossoms on them. They'd been planted poorly and both leaned at crazy angles. But they leaned in toward each other, like two yearning lovers. Simple miracle.

Record in your journal your simple miracles. Note any abstract, symbolic or metaphoric qualities, like two lovers yearning, or a farm boy glowing with future possibilities. Of course, sometimes a gamboling calf is just a gamboling calf. But sometimes it's pure bliss.

The Simple Miracle of Hearing

The best way to hear is to listen. If this sounds like a quote from the Department of Redundancy Department, consider this anonymous list of listening skills. I was humbled when I read it. I've always considered myself a good listener. I realize now, I'm a good talker. The listening part needs work. Yet, when I do listen, I learn huge, vital truths that stream out of the most unlikely mouths. And if not truths, then wonderful character stuff to use in my writing.

Listening

(Anonymous)

YOU <u>ARE NOT LISTENING</u> TO ME WHEN . . .

You do not care about me.

You say you understand before you know me well enough.

You have an answer for my problems before I've finished telling you what my problem is.

You cut me off before I've finished speaking.

You find me boring and don't tell me.

You feel critical of my vocabulary, grammar or accent.

You are dying to tell me something.

You tell me about your experience, making mine seem unimportant.

You are communicating to someone else in the room.

You refuse my thanks by saying you haven't done anything.

YOU <u>ARE LISTENING</u> TO ME WHEN . . .

You come quietly into my private world and let me be me.

You really try to understand me even if I'm not making much sense.

You grasp my point of view even when it's against your own sincere convictions.

You allow me the dignity of making my own decisions even though you think they might be wrong.

You do not take my problem from me, but allow me to deal with it in my own way.

You do not offer me solace when you sense I am not ready for it.

You give me enough room to discover for myself what is really going on.

You accept my gift of gratitude by telling me how good it makes you feel to know you have been helpful.

Get Juicy

For a full day, be in silence and simply listen. Listen to the rasp of letters coming out of the mailbox, the metallic "chok" when you snap the mailbox lid back in place. Listen to your dog lap up water, the flashy dissonance of canine toenails on tile, the thick pad of paws on carpet. Listen to the human-made world: the roar of leaf-blowers, the rumble of trucks, the angry ocean sound of distant freeway traffic. Listen to the natural world: high wind in pines, warbler glee clubs, the songs of frogs, the crunch of dry leaves, beating rain, rushing waters, buzzing wasps.

Don't forget music, lots of it. Expand your personal envelope and vary what you normally listen to. Try some reggae or sacred choral, hip-hop, R&B, country, opera, brass.

Listen.

Describe what you hear in your journal.

Before you enter silence, prepare those around you. Alert family members and coworkers to what you're going to do. Blame me: "It's this crazy creativity workshop I'm doing. Believe me, I wouldn't if I didn't have to." Scratch a note beforehand that you can pull out which reads, "I'm in silence today" (appropriate for the West Coast and Madison, Wisconsin) or "I have laryngitis" (all other areas of the country). Then stick to it.

For talky, extroverted types, this is a deep practice. I've never made it through a full day without the sound of my own voice, despite repeated efforts and extended meditation retreats. When I lose awareness, I blurt something. But I've come close and the effort is always worth it. Apart from the deep listening such an exercise entails, you'll gain the side benefit of standing a much better chance of hearing the "still small voice within," the headwaters of your creativity.

Get Juicy

Spend a week collecting voice types. Listen for the song and quality rather than the content. Think about the instruments in a symphonic orchestra, if it helps. Perhaps the voice is mellow like a French horn, bell-like as a triangle, booming like the timpani.

Moody as an oboe. Thin, nasal, and reedy like a clarinet. As hoarse as a bassoon. As strident as a snare drum, as dissonant as cymbals. Light as a violin, dark as a cello. Husky as a bass sax, silky as a flute. As full and lusty as a trombone. As piping as a piccolo.

Whispery, like dancing cottonwood leaves. Smooth and mellifluous like a late night DJ on a jazz station. Use these, find more. Collect as many as you can. You'll slick up your hearing skills and corral character types for later use in writing scenes and stories.

Get Juicy

Go to the library or music store and pick several selections of music with which you're unfamiliar—Nepali folk music, Malaysian ballads, Bulgarian women's choirs. Listen to two to three minutes of one. Turn off the music and write a story based on what you heard. Have a beginning, a middle and an end. Include characters, setting and action. Do another, to a different piece of music. Notice how different your stories are.

The Simple Miracle of Touch

We crave safe touch, abhor violent touch. Is there anything more charged than touch? A gentle touch. A clammy touch. Describe someone as silk and she's a very different character than one who is denim. Intellectual types, of whom writers are disproportionately representative, too often live from the neck up. Get down and explore textures, surfaces, temperatures, patterns. Then write about them.

Get Juicy

List twenty things you enjoy touching. Here are mine as of this moment: buttery leather, fine-grained sandpaper, my husband's beard, sanded wood, the gnarled bark of a mature Douglas fir, silk, my child's hair, my child's cheek, the smooth curve of plastic along the edge of my computer desk, my dog's warm head, new-growth fir needles, a tough-minded spruce branch, wild iris petals, rich soil, my slightly ridged right thumbnail, river rock, the curved side of my guitar, a warm coffee mug, high-thread-count sheets, the glazed coolness of my ceramic shaman's bowl.

How can you infiltrate touch into your writing? Start by listing things you enjoy touching, then incorporate the item itself or adjectives that describe it, like "nubby," "rough," "smooth," and "velvety" in your descriptions. This sort of sensory detail brings your writing alive.

Twenty Things I Like the Feel of:

1. Suede
2. cat fur
3. river rock
4. the hands of a masseuse
5. card stock
6. feathers
7. eyelashes
8. fingertips

9. *wood*

10. *bark*

11. *glass*

12. *ribbon*

13. *embroidery*

14. *newly polished nails*

15. *rose petals*

16. *Satin*

17. *ceramic*

18. *baby fingers on lips*

19. *~~Mattress~~ Tube Drum*

20. *Cymbals*

Now, write a brief description of a forest glade or a tide pool. Think texture. Use your list.

The Simple Miracle of Taste

Expand your palate. Take yourself out for ethnic food you've never eaten before. No, you may not order from the American menu. Check out what normally inedible objects taste like. (Caveat: don't try this with plants you don't know. Many are highly poisonous.) Taste rose and violet petals. Lick your own hand. Sample what your dog eats—you won't want to go there again, but it's a noble act of solidarity. Chew on a whole clove or steep some fir needle tea.

Get Juicy

Have a friend arrange a platter of different tastes—strong, unique tastes like grilled meat spices, nutmeg, fresh basil, bittersweet chocolate. With a blindfold, sample a taste. Then write a poem about it.

The Simple Miracle of Smell

A few years ago, early for a nearby rehearsal, I walked into one of the last surviving dime stores in Eugene, Oregon. I hadn't been in a dime store in years and had forgotten how distinctive their smell is. Within a few steps, memories washed over me like hard summer rain. I was with my long-dead grandma again. Even inhaled her good, comfortable smell. My grandmother used to take me into Kresge's dime store in Elkhart, Indiana on Saturday mornings for cherry Cokes. The smell of this dime store brought it all back. I nearly wept at the memory.

Smells evoke memory like nothing else I know. When I quit sugar a few years ago, I found my sense of smell grew acute. I learned to search out scents, luxuriate in them. When my boy was a baby, I loved smelling his head, the light, sour smell of amniotic fluid that lingered for months after birth, juxtaposed with the sweet smell of baby powder. I love smelling my dog's paws; the hills and rocks and sun cling to them as surely as water to a lake.

Get Juicy

Have a friend put three or four strong-smelling items like spices, herbs, cleansers and essential oils into individual glass jars or plastic containers with lids. Don't make them all pleasant.

Echinacea tincture smells god-awful, but is compelling. If using the original container, cover any labels so you can't know what's in them except by your nose. Bring out the trusty blindfold and uncap a container. Sniff deeply. Take off the blindfold and write down any memories the smell evokes. If none appear, make some up.

Suggested olfactory possibilities: Pine sol, nutmeg, fresh basil, Aqua Velva aftershave, fresh rosemary, scented geraniums, bleach, ginger, Emeraude or White Shoulders perfume, sliced onion, Vick's Vapo Rub, freshly-ground Starbucks Sumatran coffee.

The Simple Miracle of Your Sixth Sense

In his book *How to Think Like Leonardo*, Michael Gelb writes about "synthesia," the synergy of the senses where the five senses merge to form a sixth. From this sensate place, you can describe one sense in terms of another, for example, the color of sound. I think the cumulative effect of heightening all your senses results in bodily intuition, "emotional knowledge" made corporal.

Get Juicy

Put on a piece of inspiring music, like Vangelis or Schubert or Beethoven. Jazz, if that's what moves you. Crank it up. High. No, I mean *really* high. Now, lie down next to your speakers. Listen with your whole body. When you've stopped vibrating, let 'er rip and describe the experience in terms of:

Touch _Satin sheets, petals, flame on candle rain on window pane or sill, framed photo clock, envelope, lips, velvet box, puppy_

Taste dimples on a cheek, bangs, ice cream, rain drops, peppermint, love Notes, hand dipped in caramel

Sight kite in the wind, grass on back, sunlit hair, fountain, first kiss, running, twirling in breeze, head on heart, rainbow, children singing in the park, bended knee, ferris wheel, words from elders

Smell Jasmine, home-cooked meal, shampoo, cotton-candy,

_____

_____

_____

Get Juicy

Eat a complex food, like a Thai dish, and describe the taste in terms of sight, sound, feel and smell. Maybe it's a funky, crusty purple blues riff, which is a very different taste than, say, a floral, velvety fusion wave.

Get Juicy

Arrange time in a room, one you don't know well, if possible. Turn off the lights and make your way to the center of the room. Put on a blindfold. Now, spin seven times, fast. As soon as you stop, move out to explore the room, using only your nonvisual senses. You'll mostly explore by touch, but smell, taste (use your discretion here), even listen to every object you encounter. If you can hear an entire ocean in a shell, why can't you hear the universe in a chair? Don't label the objects with words, if you can help it. Just explore their qualities with your senses.

When you believe you fully know this space, turn on the lights, slip off the blindfold, sit down with your journal and write about it.

Get Juicy

Young Apache warriors in training were expected to spend a week every year blindfolded. This forces the nonvisual senses to become more acute. We tend as a species to be highly visual. That's not bad, but often we neglect our other senses. Emulate an Apache warrior for half a day. Put on a blindfold (again with the blindfold!) and continue your day. Consider walking in your yard. Prepare a meal—without knives or stoves, let's not get crazy. Clean the house. Pet the dog. Talk on the phone. Listen to music. When the blindfold comes off, write about it in your journal.

Simple miracles are all around you. They are in your fingertips, your ears, on your tongue, in your nose and eyes. Practice the first rule of creativity: pay attention. Pay close attention. Not only will attending to simple miracles juice up your creative process, it serves a highly pragmatic function. By salting your writing with specific sense details, you draw the reader in, make the writing real and immediate. Vivid.

Learning Styles

If you noticed certain sense exercises came easier than others, you probably tapped into your particular learning style. The big three are visual, auditory and kinesthetic. Often, you'll be strong in one, reasonable in another, lousy in the third. I happen to be a strong kinesthetic, with a visual second banana. Auditory? Forget it. Books on tape are lost on me. The only way I made it through school was by writing everything down. Public schools for the most part rely on visual and, to a lesser extent, auditory learning. Kinesthetics are pretty much out in the cold with no blanket, but we cope.

Once you know your learning style, you can play to its strength. If you know you're visual, you may need to flop on the couch periodically and daydream your way through a scene, relying on images to take you through rough shoals in your writing. If you're kinesthetic, you might need to move around while you write. The feel of the keyboard is probably manna on a hungry day. If you're auditory, consider using a piece of music to grapple with a tough scene. Choose carefully. If you want a dynamic scene building to an explosive climax, Ravel's "Bolero" is a much better choice than Debussy's "Prelude to Afternoon of the Faun."

Howard Gardner, famed learning theorist from Harvard, posits as many as nine intelligences:

- Musical intelligence (Mozart)

- Bodily-Kinesthetic Intelligence (Mother of Modern Dance, Martha Graham)

- Logical-Mathematical Intelligence (Stephen Hawking)

- Linguistic Intelligence (the U.N.'s U Thant)

- Spatial Intelligence (Einstein)

- Interpersonal Intelligence (Gandhi)

- Intrapersonal Intelligence (Buddhist meditation teacher, Thich Nhat Hanh)

- Naturalist Intelligence (John Muir or Charles Darwin)

If any of these smacks you up side the head and says, "So that's why I could never get through physics; I learn through music and have virtually no spatial intelligence," you'll have more information about your particular creative process.

The main learning styles are auditory, visual and kinesthetic; but consider the possibility of other ways you learn, and play to your strengths.

Get Juicy

I don't know where this exercise came from, but my writers group has been using it for years. Here's how you play. Pick a strong image or emotion. Write the word down in the middle of a clean page. Around it, draw five spokes and label them: sound, sight, smell, touch, taste. Alone or, even better, with several writer friends, free associate what the center word feels, smells, tastes, sounds and looks like. Stop after getting four or five words for each sense.

Next, free-associate through each new word, garnering yet another pool of words. Allow this level to be more abstract, even attenuated. So, for example, if the center word is "passion" and it looks "red," the word describing "red passion" might be "bold." (Passion looks red, which looks bold.) When finished, you should have forty to fifty words.

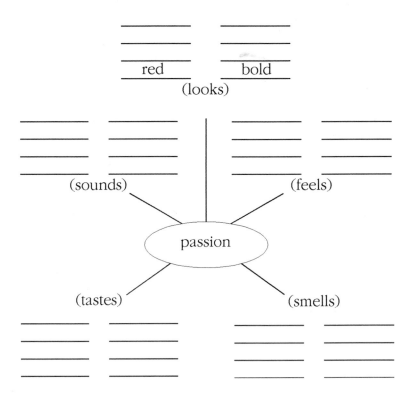

Choose a word from the following list or use your own for the center title word.

- Creativity

- Passion

- Love

- Anger

- Enlightenment

- Yearning

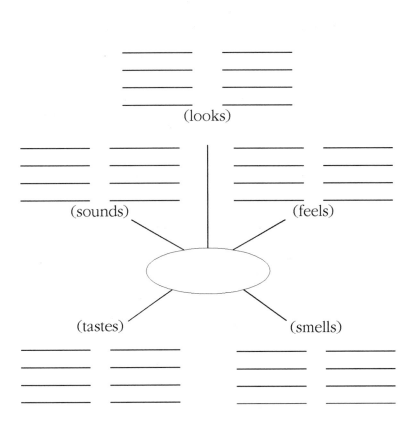

(looks)

(sounds)   (feels)

(tastes)   (smells)

Now, using this pool of words, take five minutes—no more—to write a free-verse poem with your primary word as the title. Share with a group of like-minded creative types. Trust that if you do this with a group, each poem will be wildly different, despite using the same pool of words. For example, from the same limited word pool emanating from the word "enlightenment" came these two very different offerings from students:

Waves of saffron honey lap smoothly
against the creaking wooden door.
I can finally taste the copper
Of a bell I'd previously ignored.
Clark Brook

Crashing rhythmic passions
release
sweet sticky ambrosia, silky touch
your tongue like saffron
spicy, awakening
your scent, like old wood, that's
soft from years of rubbing oils,
incense, the fire's hearth and
her ashes. Candles flaming
and soot collecting in the
bread made at my hearth.
Butter melting, fruits of sweet
ambrosia dripping with pulp
and nectar. Sticky body
golden reflecting wisdom
from our souls while always
laughing like sweating children
we kiss.
Lucretia Austell

Once you've completed the exercise, think back. From which
sense did the words flow most freely and which did you sit out

for lack of association? This helps identify whether you're kinesthetic, auditory or visual. Did you "see" your primary word readily and well, but go dry on how it "felt"? You're likely a visual and not a kinesthetic learner. If you heard it far better than you saw it, you're probably an auditory learner.

Get Juicy

Are you a kinesthetic learner? Here's a way to find out. Have a friend gather several items chosen for their unusual shapes and textures, and place them in a bag. Blindfolded, reach into the bag and take an object. Using your sense of touch, explore it completely, so completely you'll be able to pick it out from all the other items.

Once you're certain you kinesthetically know the object, put it back in the bag. Remove your blindfold and write a character study based on the object. Include the character's physical appearance (height, weight, color of hair and eyes, physique, distinguishing marks, signature walk, gesture and facial expression) and a personality profile. Top it off with the character's fondest desire and secret dreams. You don't have to use the factual reality of the object, but rather can extrapolate from your kinesthetic sense of it. If it's a soft, cuddly item, maybe your character will be like Lenny from *Of Mice and Men*. If it's a cool, angular object, perhaps you'll describe the perfect corporate raider.

When you're done with your character study, dump everything out of the bag and pick your object. If you have trouble identifying it, or found the character study daunting, there's a good chance you're not a strong kinesthetic learner. You can develop that side, if you choose, by taking dance or acting classes and using the tactile exercises available in this and other creativity books.

Get Juicy

Perhaps you're an auditory learner. Juice up by listening to what other people say. You've collected voice types by ignoring content and focusing on sound, now hone in on content. For a week, really listen to people as they talk. I'm not suggesting you inadvertently eavesdrop on someone's private conversation. There's nothing inadvertent about it. Intentionally set yourself in a situation where you can hear people talk unselfconsciously. A coffeehouse or restaurant, a bus, an airport terminal, a concert intermission. Your own home is a great place to overhear conversations, as you'll rarely get told to mind your own business.

Focus on a snippet of two to three minutes. Then, pull out your notebook and write down in as much detail as possible what was said. Include intonations, implied hidden agendas, emotional nuances, eccentric syntax, accents.

You'll likely notice human speech is unpolished and repetitive. In my misspent youth as an attorney, I saw my share of transcripts. No matter how educated they were, judges, lawyers, expert witnesses with multiple degrees all sounded like cretins when memorialized on the printed page.

You'd probably never want to replicate overheard speech in toto. We're really pretty boring unedited. But you will find gorgeous turns of phrase, jewel-like colloquialisms, verbal character brands of astonishing vividness, all for future use or current inspiration.

At a party, I once overheard a woman say, "He was a poor black dog in a bad part of town, walking down the street with a serious overbite." Apart from the street with a serious overbite— can a dentist correct that sort of thing?—which may also hold obscure metaphoric meaning, it's a fantastic line. A line to launch a thousand stories and one I'll use someday. I asked the woman if I could use it, a mere courtesy.

Listen to the speech of children. Trust me, most of the time they're nowhere near ready for "Kids Say the Darnedest Things," but they do have startling takes at times. For them, it's not a matter of creativity; they're just pedaling hard on the learning curve and doing the best they can. At two, my boy said "a pair of sleeves" to mean "shirt." After all, it was "a pair of pants." At nine he was convinced the definition of a swear word was that it served two functions: one legitimate and one to hurl as an obscenity. Considering his entire knowledge base of swear words consisted of "hell," "damn," and "asshole," it made perfect sense.

He gave me fresh perspectives and made me wonder what other words might be employed to serve double duty. "Tweak" could have its dictionary meaning as well as a street meaning for "citified cousin of a twerp." "Spit" could mean both "expectorate" and "the turd of one who lisps." The possibilities are endless. Ask a kid.

If these auditory exercises leave you cold, there's every chance you're not primarily an auditory learner.

Get Juicy

Maybe you're a visual learner. In a large envelope, collect compelling images you come across in magazines. The images may attract, repel, confront or comfort you; but you are drawn to them for some not necessarily conscious reason. When you have a gracious plenty, throw them down, choose one that pulls you at the moment, preferably for a mysterious or baffling reason—forget "shoulds"— and write a story based on the image. Perhaps the image suggests the setting, the characters or even the story line.

Say your image is a pristine mountain peak, this time in winter. Maybe one of your characters could be an extreme adventure buff and the other a wildly competitive type who always has to be number one, and they're fighting over who gets to ski down first. Or maybe the adventure buff is married to a queasy, fearful character who, now that they've struggled all the way up, is too frightened to go down. Or raise the stakes. Maybe the two have become lost during a winter climb and have a single space blanket between them. Who gets it and so survives?

Whether this exercise was more or less comfortable than the auditory ones should give you some clue as to whether you're primarily auditory or visual. If you're still not sure, here are a few more exercises to help you determine your learning style.

Get Juicy

Listen to a radio program for five minutes. Write down in as much detail as you can what you heard. How many details were you able to supply? Not many? You're probably not a strong auditory learner. More details than anybody wants to hear—my mother-in-law can spend forty-five minutes telling me about a half hour soap—and you're probably an auditory learner.

Get Juicy

Speaking of soap operas, watch one for five minutes with the sound muted. Write about what happened. Hopeless without the sound? You're probably not strongly visual. Off and running with a detailed storyline? You're visual.

Get Juicy

This exercise has three parts.

1. Have a friend audiotape a randomly selected scene from a play you don't know. Listen to it, then write a synopsis of what transpired.

2. Read a scene, again selected at random from a play you don't know. Write a brief synopsis of the scene without referring back to the script.

3. Finally, perform a different, two-character scene either with a friend, or by yourself, changing your voice and physicality for each character. Once completed, write a synopsis.

If you found reading the scene more effective than acting it out, you're likely a visual learner. If acting it out gave you greater understanding, you're probably a kinesthetic learner. If you got the most out of listening to someone else read it, you're auditory.

The benefit of knowing your learning style isn't simply fodder for your creative process. It can also significantly improve the quality of your writing. You can play to your strengths, sure; but just as importantly, you can nourish your weaknesses. If you know you live through your eyes, customarily ignoring auditory or kinesthetic cues, you can intentionally make up for it by going back over your writing and inserting sound details. What does your protagonist hear as she's sliding down the mountain? What does she feel; just how cold is it out there? If you live from your ears, rewrite for textures and temperatures, sights and images. If you're a kinesthetic, weave in the sights and sounds you may have ignored on first draft.

Cross-pollination

No one, and most certainly not an artist, lives in a vacuum. Environmental author, Paul Hawken, summed up what quantum physicists and Eastern religions have long known: "Everything is connected . . . no one thing can change by itself." If you're limiting your life to a nine-to-five job and sitcoms, it will show in your work. Conversely, every creative act you take nourishes your creative whole, greens a field that may have been lying fallow. Inspire yourself. Do something involving your senses that you've never done before. You don't have to be good at it; this is creative play that incorporates all learning styles.

Get yourself some clay. Squish it around. Get yourself some paints. Indulge. Get yourself a drum. Go wild. Now, write about it. About the heft of the clay, the sensual spread of the paint, the vividness of the turquoise and how it reminds you of the Sea of Cortez on an exuberant day. How the beating of the drum thundered glory. Celebrate the song of yourself. I am wild child, I am, I am, I am that I am, a footfall of god. A cobalt streak in a pure white sky.

Get Juicy

List ten artsy things you think might be fun. Metal sculpture. Flamenco. African marimba. Woodcarving. Calligraphy. Whatever appeals to you. Choose one and sign up for a class in it. Consider doing at least one a year. If you're having trouble thinking of something, consult the list on pages 64-65. My students came up with a bodacious abundance of fun things to try.

1. _____

2. _____

3. _____

4. _____

5. _____

6. _____

7. _____

8. _____

9. _____

10. _____

Arts

Clog dancing

Jazz dance

Modern dance

Square dance

Folk dance

Line dance

Flamenco

African dance

Belly dance

Hula

Ballet

Origami

Paper making

Puppetry

Mask making

Calder mobile making

Oil painting

Watercolor

Drawing

Pottery

Sculpture

Welding

Printmaking

Lithography

Chinese brush painting

Weaving

Embroidery

Needlepoint

Knitting

Woodcarving

Twig furniture

Folk art on wood furniture

Acting class

Voice-over

Improvisation

Community theater

Stenciling

Quilting

Soft sculpture

Found sculpture

Jewelry making

Cloisonné

Writing classes

Song-writing

Voice lessons

Violin lessons

Piano, French horn, clarinet lessons

Flute, trumpet, oboe lessons

Take up the sax or guitar

Adventure

Hot air ballooning	Golf
Scuba diving	Skydiving
Horseback riding	Yoga
Hang gliding	Skiing
Parasailing	Sweat lodge
Playing with dolphins	Build a tree house
Swimming with Manatees	Exotic train trips
Sailing	Cruise Alaska
White water rafting	Mountain climbing
Sea kayaking by moonlight	Rock climbing
Canoeing a wild river	Hiking the wilderness

Look at the list you've made: what do your choices tell you about your learning style?

Wrestling the Demons

Some creative artists grow up perfectly well-adjusted. They never lack confidence, accept rejection with ease, and always maintain a cheerful, positive outlook about their work and their lives. I've never met these people. The artists I've met have struggled. With self-doubt and its evil twin, perfectionism. With depression and addictions. With rejection.

Notice I used the past tense "struggled." Many artists have overcome these creative demons and their work is richer for it. I am not saying you have to be a "tortured artist" to create. I'm all for easy, if it's true. So if you've never had to deal with any of these issues, Bravo! Skip this section and go on to week five. But if you suspect any of these demons abrades your creative soul like psychic sandpaper, read on.

Perfectionism

If there is a core addiction that plagues writers, I suspect it is perfectionism. God knows we have plenty of others, but for now, I want us to look perfectionism hard in the face.

"What if I'm not good enough?" Every writer who's ever lived has wondered at one time or another whether she has what it takes. One of Leonardo da Vinci's final journal entries before his death bemoaned the many projects he'd left unfinished and questioned whether he'd accomplished anything at all in his life. The greatest genius in history and he questioned his worth.

A tree doesn't question itself—am I green enough? Am I growing fast enough? What will the other trees in the forest think of me? A tree is what it is. It lives and breathes and grows. It is the way of the tree, its nature. So, too, we do well not to judge ourselves, censor, second-guess, or critique our creative output.

Does this mean we don't strive for excellence, that we throw any old thing down on the page and call it finished? Of course not. We edit and refine and give voice until our work gleams. But if we are so paralyzed by perfectionism that we can't get the first draft actually written, what good is it?

Julia Cameron maintains the worth of our work isn't our business. That's for the critics and editors and agents and reading public to determine. I don't fully agree—our internal critic can come in handy during re-writes—but I think the notion of relinquishing the censor during the creative process is not only sound, but imperative.

We create because it is the way of our people. We don't do well when we aren't creating. Be like a tree. Fulfill your nature. Create and don't worry about whether it's "good enough."

There's a phrase in theater, often spoken tongue-in-cheek but with more than a grain of truth, that's said when someone is obsessing about a flawed detail, to the time-consuming detriment of everyone around him, "Don't worry about it; we'll fix it with the lights." Meaning, just move on. Don't fixate on why it won't be good enough, why it's not working, why you ever bothered to get out of bed this lifetime. Make it as best you can and *move on*.

It's the same with writing. "We'll fix it in rewrites" are words to live by if you're stuck. You may be someone who pores over every word of every sentence and that's great, as long as the words are getting down, albeit slowly. But if you're frozen on a blank page, fearful of looking like a fool and you haven't written a word in a month of Tuesdays, you're using perfectionism as self-flagellation.

Anything worth doing is worth doing mediocrely. Maybe this is the mud before the gold. Maybe this is the gold and you just need to sift through it a little more. Write it down. Keep moving. You can always throw it out later, but don't be too quick about that; bad moods pass and what you've created may look considerably better tomorrow.

The playwright, Lillian Hellmann, set aside a specific time each day for negativity. For precisely one hour every afternoon, she wailed out her anguish and despair. At the end of the hour, she emotionally dusted herself off and carried on with her life. This kind of compartmentalization may be precisely what we require as creative artists.

During your creating time, and that means any rough draft, agree to dump your inner critic. When perfectionism pops up, simply notice it and let it go. You can always pick it up later, but right now there's no place for it. If you want, you can let your critic rage in rewrites; although even there, it's important to step back and give yourself enough emotional distance to not take it personally. Imagine you're doing an editing project for a stranger.

During the creating itself, ban perfecitonism. I mean "perfectionism," but I'll fix it in rewrites.

Get Juicy

We're always anthropomorphizing, ascribing human qualities to nonhuman beings and objects. Try it the other way to rid yourself of some all-too-human doubt. Cast yourself as just another simple miracle in nature, which, of course, is what you are. Choose something nonhuman, something that would no more doubt itself than sing "My Country 'Tis of Thee" under water. What are you? Find an image from nature and elaborate.

Look for the metaphors in the image that inform your life. Be sure they're positive—this is important. Maybe you're a graceful live oak, extending gnarled branches over great space, providing shade and the beauty of dappled light. As a tree, you are strong, able to weather any blow. Beautiful and graceful in age. You have the dignity of your trunk, the beauty of your foliage, the flippant silliness of squirrels scampering through your branches.

Perhaps you are a river that flows over every obstacle, a shell that holds the entire sea within its pearl-pink confines, a kite that bobs from breeze to breeze in clear sunlight. Stretch it out. If you're a river, how far do you flow? Where is your headwater and into what great sea do you empty? If you're stuck, consider these: a great blue heron, a meadowlark's song, a bonfire, an ice storm after the sun comes out, a panda's sigh, an apple orchard on a crisp October afternoon, a waterfall, a great wind, a canyon of voluptuous white boulders. What are you?

Depending on your learning style, you may want to do this visually.

If you're kinesthetic, you may want to dance your nature totem, imagining its textures, smells, sights and sounds, feeling what it is to be that entity. If you're auditory, listen to the song your totem makes—the rustle of leaves, the glissando of water.

When you've chosen your nature image and teased out its positive metaphors, write a haiku about it. A haiku is a Japanese poem written in three lines of five, seven, five syllables respectively, all centered around a single image from nature. Generally lyrical, they don't have to be. Witness these haikus about dogs I received in my e-mail this morning:

I sound the alarm!

Mailman, come to kill us all

Look! Look! Look! Look! Look!

I am your best friend,

Now, always, and especially

When you are eating.

Author unknown

Remember, it doesn't have to be perfect.

Find a picture of your totem image and stick it on the wall in your writing area. The next time self-doubt rears its ugly back, look at that picture and ask: does this river or tree or rock or song ever doubt itself?

Then, neither will I.

I am an Oak Tree
Standing Strong in Wind
Letting Go Easy

I am a Diamond
Shining in the Dark
No Matter the Grit

Get Juicy

This exercise combines deep relaxation techniques with neurolinguistic programming to anchor the state, so you can return to it when you want. In a contented, relaxed state, it's hard to rage, "It's not good enough!"

Turn off the phone. Lie down, arms at your sides, feet uncrossed. Note any sensate awareness, the feel of the floor under your back, the sound of the heat pump, the taste of your own mouth. Forget the to-do list that awaits you. Forget the fight you had with your kid over breakfast, the errands you've got to run before five. Release everything and let yourself be. There's an old Buddhist meditation phrase that's helpful to calm a caffeine mind: "There's nowhere to go and nothing to do." Ultimately, it's as true as true gets, when you think about it.

Close your eyes. Follow your breath. Don't try to change it, just allow it to come naturally. Peacefully. After a few moments, allow your eyes to become relaxed and rested. Imagine a soft cloud of relaxation covering your eyes. Let it drape you in relaxation. Take as much time as you need. There's nowhere to go and nothing to do.

Now this warm, fluffy blanket of relaxation is covering your eyebrows and forehead—let them relax. Now your cheeks and jaw, covered with a warm cloud of relaxation; let them droop, sag. Allow your mouth to relax, perhaps even open a little bit.

Take that fluffy cloud of relaxation and send it up over the back of your head and down your neck. Feel it relax every muscle. Send it down your upper back. Down your chest and into your arms and hands. Feel the warmth in your hands. They may even tingle a bit.

Continue this warm cloud of relaxation into your midriff, belly and lower back. Feel it warm your hips and thighs as it flows downward, downward, soft and warm. Let it cover your knees and calves, send it down into your feet and your toes. Every part of you, deeply, deeply relaxed.

If you find any discomfort remaining anywhere in your body, breathe that fluffy, warm cloud of relaxation into that place slowly and gently until it relaxes.

Gently come back to your breath. Don't try to change it, just notice it. It may be slower and deeper now. Follow it.

When you feel completely relaxed, without any effort allow a comforting word, image, sound or sensation to bubble up from your depths. Perhaps it's the image you found to ward off perfectionism, or perhaps it's a single, meaningful word, or simply a feeling that moves through and caresses you. Whatever it is for you, allow it to bubble up and repeat effortlessly, endlessly and gently throughout your being. With every repetition, you find yourself growing more and more relaxed, more and more content, more and more at peace. You're home.

Now, anchor this state of deep relaxation by softly pressing a finger against your thigh. Know that whenever you wish to return to this pleasant state of relaxation, all you need to do is repeat your comforting image, sound, word or sensation. Touch your thigh to deepen the state. Now, very gently return to this room.

Depression

Research indicates considerably greater incidence of depression, especially manic depression, among highly creative people. Maybe the genetic biochemistry that breeds creativity also lies in wait with the grey mist that descends like a shroud when you least expect it. It isn't rational and it is real. I'm not talking about misery that comes from specific reasons—deep loss, death, rejection by a loved one, spirit-abrading poverty. I'm talking about the blues that appear out of nowhere for no apparent reason, leaving you with the gaping question of what do you do when you have it all and it isn't enough. You've created a good life filled with meaning, friends, creativity, spirituality—done every thing you know to do, and it's still not enough.

While it sounds as clichéd as it is, it's also true that, "This too shall pass." Gratitude will return. Colors will grow vivid again. Your creative work will flow once more. Seasons of darkness must by their nature give way to seasons of light. Sinking down in depression may actually be an artist's way of moving into strange and restive waters we cannot consciously give ourselves to, but which are requisite for the depth implicit in a creative life.

What if the emptiness at our core that we fear so much is some sort of divine nothingness, the very stuff of enlightenment? There's precious little you can do about it, so why not embrace the shadow?

The words don't always have to be glum, "Life is real; life is earnest." Often, only humor will do, even if it's the gallows variety.

Have courage. Keep faith. In yourself and in your work. Even when the well seems driest, write through it. Write, "I have nothing to say," if you must, over and over, but move your fingers, speak your word, leak the emptiness all over the page.

And consider antidepressants.

Okay, it was tossed in as a joke, but there's truth just below. Professional help may be needed. If you can't seem to get a handle on it, get help. You wouldn't try to treat your own diabetes; why would you think you can treat your own depression? For some of us, occasional depression's an old friend, and we feel comfortable slogging through to the other side. But if that other side is too long coming, go for assistance. The only shame is in letting it rule and ruin your life. If depression is giving you something other than misery, if it's taking you down to a level you need to explore, so be it. May you ride the swift wind and land softly. But if it's savaging you for no purpose—I know, everything serves some purpose . . . but enough may be enough—get off the ride. No blame. No shame.

We live in a tough culture with an excess of material abundance and a dearth of spiritual wealth. Consumerism can only take you so far—about to the corner. After that, you're stranded by the side of the road with no gas can and barely a thumb to hitch. Creation is spiritual and fills our psychic emptiness, the empty hole lodged in so many of our bellies. Anything else you can do to feed the spiritual component of your life is all to the good, both as an artist and a human being. Find a church, worship in a forest, open to awe and wonder and deep gratitude at the on-going miracles present in every day. It doesn't have to be "religious." Imagine something as powerful and useful as the sun—it's enough to boggle the spirit. And a five-year-old's laugh? Forget about it! Such magnificence can't be possible, yet there it is.

When is it incubation and when is it depression? And what about the buzzy manic phase, if it comes? Sometimes, we walk a fine line as creative folk. Salvador Dali said, "The only difference between me and a madman is that I am not mad." If you've studied his life and work, you know his declaration is subject to dispute. But no one can question the unmitigated brilliance of his vision or the masterfulness of his technique. An openness to the odd detail—the vivid blue shadow—the frankly strange sensibility is what distinguishes writers from typists.

Social psychologist, Susan K. Perry notes in her book, *Writing in Flow*, the close similarities in mental processes between an artistic and schizophrenic mind. The comparison is sobering. Must we be mad to create, or at least slide down the razor blade at its edge? Must we be drunks, sexual obsessives, addicts hell-bent for leather to keep the words flowing?

Here's the short answer: no. While depression, addictions and perfectionism often plague creative types, we write in spite—not because—of these afflictions. If anything, overcoming these blocks rather than surrendering to them becomes the spur to our creative output.

I've created for lots of reasons. A big one was to heal. No matter how splintered I felt, when I created I was whole. In her book, *Writing as a Way of Healing*, Louise DeSalvo notes the link between creativity and healing, how to write yourself well.

> "The writing process, no matter how much time we devote to it, contains a tremendous potential for healing . . . Through writing, we cultivate the quality of absorption—becoming deeply immersed in our work. This quiets us and calms us while, paradoxically, engaging us, whether we are writing about pleasant moments or continuing psychic pain.

> "Writing regularly fosters resilience—a quality that enables people subjected to difficulties to thrive despite them . . .

> "This is because as we write we become observers—an important component of developing resilience. We regard our lives with a certain detachment and distance when we view them as subjects to describe and interpret. We reframe the problems in our lives as challenges as we ask ourselves how to articulate what is on our minds in a way that will make sense."

Connie May Fowler, author of *When Women Had Wings* and many other beautiful novels, had what can only be described as a tough childhood, yet she has used her childhood wounds to create magic on pages that inspirit and uplift us. Stories that don't shy from grit, yet ultimately glow. She wouldn't be the same person, have the same depth, without the pain she's known.

No matter what happens in your life, no matter how bad, how painful, how deep the loss, do your best to struggle to a place of acceptance, even gratitude. Life's pain is the straw from which we spin creative gold.

I've had two great gifts in my life: alcoholism and chronic illness. Before you count me out as a masochist, let me explain. Without having been forced into recovery from full-blown alcoholism twenty years ago, I would never have gotten to know myself so well nor have gained the breadth and help of a deep spiritual path. Without many years of chronic illness, I never would have known true quiet or understood priorities.

The deeper the pain, the deeper the healing. And the deeper the healing, the deeper your creative work. In a way I only fuzzily understand, being forced to embrace life's sorrow down to the marrow freed me. Broken open, without the usual props of credentials and accomplishments, my weighty ego dissolved like mist in sun.

I struggled all my life with self-worth, yet when I had nothing to show but my unadorned self, only then did I know self-acceptance. I was worthy for no other reason than I drew breath. It was a remarkable epiphany. Words like "vulnerability" and "risk" became moot. In this most vulnerable of all states, one becomes invulnerable, impervious to external yammering, secure in the simple miracle of existence.

I don't recommend getting sick to discover your rightful place in the world, but I do recommend using all the grist given you as fuel for the flames in which you forge your inner steel. And never assume the grist is "bad." It's tough to see the big picture in the middle of all the flying chaff.

When my dad served in World War II, he was a medic with the rank of Corporal. His unit hiked through the Italian Alps one night, the starless midnight so inky black each man had to put his hand on the shoulder of the man in front of him and move by feel.

Suddenly, they heard the shriek of incoming artillery shells.

Misjudging the depth of the ditch beside him, my father leapt for cover. He twisted his leg as he fell.

After the shelling, the unit stopped for the night. The next morning, my dad tried to continue, but it became clear his injury was significant enough he couldn't keep up. His superior officer told him to report to the field hospital, a mile back the way they'd come.

In great pain, he limped away, cursing his luck. He turned back for a look. In the dawn light he was just able to make out the silhouettes of his buddies cresting the ridge.

It was the last time he saw them.

On the other side of the ridge, my father's unit was captured by an enemy platoon. All the noncoms of my father's rank were lined up and shot.

Getting injured had seemed like a tough break. Not.

Never presume you know the whole picture. What happens to us may be bad; it may be good.

Write about all of it. Some words you may never show to the public or even another human being, but words are powerful. They can free what has been caged, heal what has been sick.

Addictions

I've written drunk and I've written sober and sober is better. I've taken care of myself physically, spiritually and emotionally and I've let myself go to hell; and healthy is better, clearer, more focused, more creative. Yes, Virginia, there is a muse and it doesn't live in a bottle. It lives in the clean air of a centered being.

When you're running hard from addictions, be they food, drink, work, drugs, gambling or sexual relationships, you're spending enormous amounts of energy on the addiction—on protecting your source, on denying its power over you, on making excuses for the devastation it's wreaking in your life—energy that could be going into your creative work. Don't confuse being frazzled and raw with artistic sensibility. It isn't. It's illness.

Addiction can be self-medicating. I'm not saying addictions don't work. They do. For a while. Until they don't. Then they turn on you hard, snarling teeth bared, going for the jugular. And they will kill unless you fight back.

Alcohol addiction's easy to spot: have you had blackouts from drinking? Have you ever lost predictability, said you were only going to have a certain number of drinks, then were unable to stick to that limit? Huge red flags flapping wildly in the wind. For any addiction: has the activity adversely affected your work? Your relationships? Your self-respect? Tell the truth: are you out of control around the activity, compelled to do it when you don't really want to? Do it unconsciously, then rage at yourself afterwards?

I know how those shadowy early days of struggle feel when you first admit the booze or the food or whatever the compulsion is has gotten away from you, has ridden hard over your fresh green soul and left it a trampled, sorry thing. The admission is rarely clean and often comes in tangled sidesteps.

When I was twenty-nine, I looked great on paper. I was a rising star attorney who'd graduated in the top ten percent of my class, had developed a strong professional reputation and often starred in local theater productions. I was also rotting away inside from drink. One night, I got drunk and flipped my car. I came to with the taste of blood in my mouth. I smelled gas, knew I had to get out fast. Upside down, I struggled with the seat belt, fumbled for the window crank. It wouldn't budge. I crawled to the passenger side, was able to force the window down, and crawled out. I had run just a few steps when the car burst into flames.

Even for a drama queen, the message was abundantly clear. I had a problem. A big problem. And I got the message. Except it took me five months and dozens of drunks before I actually walked my butt in to get help. So, be patient with yourself, but not so patient you don't do something about it. The difference in the quality of your life and your creative work will be night and day.

It has taken twenty years and huge amounts of work, but I bless my alcoholism every day. Without it, I never would have known myself so well, never would have found spiritual and creative fulfillment.

Working the Grist

If the Pollyanna platitudes have you ready to gag, suck it up. I've tried to cultivate a properly sophisticated, cynical attitude at different times in my life, but the universe kept laughing and telling me, "Everything that happens to you is for a good reason, whether you can make sense of it or not." Every problem you've walked through, every loss you've borne has given you greater strength as a writer. Every dark breathes light.

I have a friend whose life makes the most melo-dramatic soap opera look like a stroll in a garden. A horrible accident left her brilliant, fifteen-year-old daughter brain injured. My friend was by her daughter's side as she spent years relearning to walk and talk; together they weathered awful, violent phases. Meanwhile, my friend's only other child, a son, had to go into forced drug rehab and was ultimately diagnosed with psychotic bipolar disorder. The woman has been through hell and gone.

But she brought something back with her. During the dark years of struggle with her daughter, she was dismayed to find virtually no literature for parents about what to expect and how to cope. Because of new medications, children who normally would have died are now surviving, but general lay information hasn't caught up. My friend decided to write a book about her daughter's experience and its effect on the family system, including her son. A nationally prominent agent loved the idea and asked her—twice—to submit a proposal. My friend's dark night of the soul has transformed into guidance for other parents, not to mention the beginning of a much-desired writing career. She had a choice; she could become bitter and wail at an unfeeling sky, or let the experience soften her, tenderize her soul so she could serve it up to others.

You're a writer. Every experience you have, no matter how horrific, nourishes the richness of your soul, the authenticity of your voice. Spiritual teacher Ram Dass says our work here on earth is to let our hearts break. And break and break and break. To let in the pain and angst and horror and give back compassion.

Just because you've lived a life other than the one portrayed on "Donna Reed," does that mean you have something to say? Yes. There is no one on the planet with your perspective; you are unique. Paradoxically, expressing your truth, even when it's painful, may warm others who struggle and think they're alone, call to them, hold them in hands they didn't know existed.

Will what you write be published? Probably. I'm a big believer that there is a market for everything. It may not win the Pulitzer Prize (unless of course it does), but it may be the very thing to fill that quarter page in the Homeowners' Association newsletter this month. Start where you are. But don't limit yourself. The first nonfiction article I ever wrote ran in *Sports Illustrated*; nobody had told me it was impossible for beginners to crack top national markets. Have all my articles made the big-time? Hardly. And the rejection slips could paper a small bathroom. All right, a moderate-sized bathroom. I'm going for a healthy ballroom. Which leads us to . . .

Dealing with Rejection and Writer's Block

If you're not getting rejection slips, you're either not getting enough work out or not aiming high enough. Rejection slips are a way of life for writers. Never assume a rejection reflects on the quality of your writing. A rejection slip often means the piece you submitted wasn't the right fit for the editor, either because she doesn't handle that type of material, or because she does but the timing was wrong; perhaps she recently worked with a similar piece and didn't need a duplicate. The way to avoid these rejections is to thoroughly research your targeted publication. Read several issues, know the tone and topics its editors prefer. Learn the fine art of killer queries.

A rejection could also mean the editor threw your piece into a slush pile unread because it was improperly formatted. Always submit your work with the highest professional standards. If you don't know formatting rules for your particular genre, find out. Writer's Digest puts out a book on how to format everything from novel manuscripts to nonfiction queries.

A rejection slip can mean a lot of things, none of which have to do with the quality of your writing. I once directed a two-person play that called for a geeky, awkward woman. A lovely young woman whose acting I greatly admired auditioned for the part, and I tried with all my imagination to envision her in the role. I wanted very much to work with her. Ultimately, though, she was simply too good-looking and graceful to be believable in that role. Because it was a university situation, I was able to tell her why she'd been rejected; but in many situations, with casting calls like auction day at the Chicago stockyards, she'd never have known. So, if you're rejected, just assume your piece is too damn good-looking.

The best rejections are those where the editor has taken the time to pencil a line or two on the publication's form letter. The same letter that reads, "Because of the volume of material we receive, we are unable to personally comment." Cherish these and give them a prominent place in your rejection hall of fame. Sometimes, they'll contain advice on how to make the piece better, a gift you'd normally have to pay for. Often, they'll offer an encouraging word, water on a thirsty day. For these rejection slips, you may want to resubmit at a different time, or send some other piece, directing it to the same editor or agent.

Aim to receive at least five rejections in a single day. That means your output is sufficiently large to hit with something. In the *I Ching*, one of my favorite phrases is, "Perseverance furthers." I used to hate it. I'm a Gemini and like my results quick and flashy. Now, as doddering middle age overtakes me, I recognize the wisdom inherent in that little aphorism. "Perseverance furthers." It's not about luck. It's not about inspiration. It's not even about talent. It's about perseverance, a willingness to learn your craft and write from an authentic place.

Stories abound about the nosebleed number of rejections famous authors received for works that turned out to be masterpieces or at the least best sellers. If they can survive rejection, so can you.

Don't be bowled over by rejections. Give a heart-felt "hoo-ha" and carry on. Get something else out that same day, if at all possible. If the rejection is a big one—an agent you've just done massive rewrites for, a movie option that looked promising—a two- or three-minute snit may be in order, but don't carry it around with you.

An ancient tale tells of two monks traveling. When they reached a river, they found a woman desperate to cross, but she couldn't withstand the raging current. One of the monks picked up the woman and carried her over, set her down on the other side and went on. Shocked—these monks were under vows to have no physical contact with women—the other monk hurried to catch up. A mile down the trail, he turned to the monk who had transported the woman and said, "I can't believe you touched that woman! What will our teacher say?" The first monk looked at him with amusement and replied, "Are you still carrying that woman? I left her at the river."

Leave your rejection angst at the river.

Writer's Block

Been there. Done that. I have a pal in my writers' group who produces a prodigious output of short stories and articles. Constantly. Month in, month out. Never at a loss for words. The woman is a machine. I don't hate her, but I want to know what she's on. Actually, she doesn't even do caffeine, maybe that's her secret.

For the rest of us mortals, writer's block is real. Suddenly, the words that flew off your pen or keyboard last week defy you this week, give you the cold, silent treatment and you can't for the life of you think what you've done wrong. You're doing everything right: writing without censoring, with an open, beginner's mind, following the most important philosophical maxim for a writer, "get your butt in the chair," honoring any little writing rituals you've established. And you're getting nothing. Day after day, the blank stare of your computer screen makes you itchy and there seems to be zip you can do about it.

When the woolly dries strike, use this arsenal.

Best Ten Ways to Beat Writer's Block

1. **Seek Your People**. Take a writing class, join a writers' group and attend the meetings, go to a writers' conference. In a word or seven, get in the company of other writers. Lean back and cook in their juice for a while until you regenerate your own.

2. **Seek Inspiration**. Read a good writing book. Anything by Julia Cameron or Natalie Goldberg, *Bird by Bird* by Annie LeMott, *Poem Crazy* by Susan Wooldridge, *A Writer's Book of Days* by Judy Reeve, or *Self-Editing for the Fiction Writer* by Renni Browne and Dave King. Subscribe to a writers' magazine, like *Writers Digest*, or *The Writer*, or *Poets and Writers*.

3. **Get Physical**. Exercise every day. Speed walk, bike, swim, dance. Play tennis, take an aerobics class, practice Tai Chi. Do something. Every day. This is also requisite treatment for depression.

4. **Free Journal**. Every day. Whether or not you have anything to say. Write, "blah blah blah" if you have to, until something comes out. Describe simple miracles, if nothing else.

5. **Get Yourself Out in Nature**. Go to a beautiful spot. Kayak a wild and scenic river. Ramble a rose garden. Hike a trail. Somehow, somewhere, get out in nature. This has never failed me. You'll almost certainly come back refreshed.

6. **Meditate.** Or pray. Or do some contemplative practice. It will calm and center and revive you.

   Good introductory meditation primers include *Seeking the Heart of Wisdom* by Joseph Goldstein and Jack Kornfield, *A Path with Heart* by Jack Kornfield, and *Peace Is Every Step* by Thich Nhat Hanh. Or simply sit quietly, eyes closed, in a comfortable position and follow your breathing. Don't try to change it; simply follow it and, when your mind drifts, notice it's drifted and gently return it to the breath. Do this for twenty minutes once or twice a day.

   A comparable practice in the Christian tradition is called Centering Prayer. For this practice, read a sacred text, like the Bible, with soft, receptive eyes, and find a particular word that touches you. Let the word enter your heart. Sit quietly with your eyes closed and gently repeat that word in your mind for several minutes.

   Here's a quick meditative technique I used to birth a baby at forty without so much as an aspirin. Try it right now: Focus your concentration on a fixed point—it doesn't matter what it is, so long as it's stationary—then breathe in through your nose on a slow count of four, out through your mouth on a slow count of five. (The entire cycle should take six to ten seconds.) Repeat, breathing in a continuous circle, in, out, in, out, without pausing between the in- and out-breaths, for several breaths.

Check in. Bet you're feeling calmer than you were when you started. This is basic LaMaze breathing, and I don't know of a more effective tool for calming, dealing with pain, or working yourself through stuck places. This breathing brings you home when you've strayed. Try it the next time something upsets you.

7. **Read Good Writers**. Hit the library and browse. Circle book reviews. Check selections from readers' clubs that look interesting, and track them down. Ask friends for their all-time favorite reads. (Mine is *A Hundred Years of Solitude*. I've read it three times, incredible for a new-stimuli-seeking Gemini.)

8. **Cross-Pollinate**. Try dancing, painting, photography, clay, acting. Pull out the arts-and-crafts box and see what falls out. Take an improvisation workshop at your local adult learning center. Go line-dancing. List twenty fun things you always wanted to try, then do at least one every year. Check page 64-65 for ideas. Get yourself to a gallery, to a dance recital, to a concert. Dive into somebody else's creative juice. You'll come up with a deep, inspired breath.

9. **Trust Your Own Process**. You're incubating. Even if you're procrastinating for some deep-seated, obstructive reason, you're still incubating. You'll be back. Keep faith.

10. **Remember to Laugh**. Humor is so important it deserves its own section.

Humor

Humor can pull you out of the doldrums, fill the well, move you through the blues. Not just in your writing but in your everyday existence. Life holds ineffable sweetness, even in sorrow, if only we can hold it lightly. Humor gives us a feathery vessel for doing that, a smiling receptivity. Humor is a way of being, a willingness to see the glow amid the gloom, the horse laugh in the horror.

Reasons abound why laughter is good for you. Research shows it improves health and reduces stress. Norman Cousins claims he healed himself of a terminal disease by holing himself up in a hotel room with a stack of funny books and the entire collection of Marx Brothers movies.

Humor can connect you to people and transform a difficult communication. Remember a time when you felt so uptight you thought you might implode? Suddenly something tickled you. You laughed out loud and tension fled. It works the same way on the page.

Most important, humor breeds creativity. If you're feeling blocked, one good laugh can turn it around. Laughter is an instantaneous freedom from conformity's confines, an open window to another perspective. Humor makes bearable what otherwise could grind us down to a dusty heap of pencil shavings.

One of my most important criterion for choosing a mate was whether he possessed a sense of humor. Mind you, you've got to give a guy a chance. I almost wrote off my husband after our first date because he didn't laugh at my favorite joke.

Okay, I'll tell you.

George Bernard Shaw was lying on his deathbed in a coma, surrounded by grieving friends. One friend peered down and said, "I think he's gone." Another friend said, "Check his feet. The feet always get cold when they die." At that point, Shaw, with tremendous effort, raised himself up and said, "Joan of Arc's didn't," then fell back dead.

I find this hysterically funny, but my future husband looked at me as if I'd grown an extra nose. Ergo, my decision he most certainly wasn't the one. Only later did I find out that: a) he didn't know Joan of Arc was burned at the stake and b) he didn't know George Bernard Shaw wrote the play *Saint Joan*. Once I illuminated him, he saw why it was funny and I fell in love.

Humor allows you to contemplate deep, philosophical questions like:

- If toast always lands butter-side down and cats always land on their feet, what happens if you strap toast on the back of a cat and drop it?

- Why isn't the word "phonetic" spelled with an "f"?

- Was it somebody's idea of a cruel joke to put an "s" in "lisp"?

- What was the best thing before sliced bread?

- If you're sending somebody Styrofoam, what do you pack it in?

These aren't original. I'm one of those people who can't remember a joke to save my life. I can memorize entire scripts, but jokes fly out of my head as soon as I hear them. I love reading them, though, so when my friends send me jokes on the Internet I print them out. Since my mind is often like a big wedge of Brie left out in the sun, I get to enjoy them over and over. They're always new to me—I have a good memory; it's just short.

Besides using humor to work through blocks, consider salting your work with it. Virtually any type of writing benefits from leavening, so long as it's done with respect for your reader. For example, you wouldn't use slapstick as the opening to a tragedy; that sets your reader up for an abashed fall when he discovers he's reading a tear-wrencher rather than a belly-laugher. Yet even tragedies benefit from irony or wit.

Types of Humor

Consider the several variants of humor you can apply in your work.

SLAPSTICK

Physical humor à la the Three Stooges, Keystone Kops, Jim Carrey. Broad, practical jokes fall into this category, like the ever-popular Whoopee Cushion, which, by the way, was the original stage name Whoopi Goldberg laid on her agent—accent on the Cu-SHONE—but was talked out of.

FARCE

Also broad, but relies more on words, e.g., the Marx Brothers, who combined slapstick with farce, or early Neil Simon. Any British play whose set has at least three doors is almost certainly a bedroom farce.

SATIRE

Using exaggeration, this humor makes fun of something or someone. Think the *Washington Review*, the San Francisco Mime Troupe, *Saturday Night Live*.

PARODY

A specific form of satire that makes fun of a particular genre or style, e.g., the movie *Airplane*, parodying disaster movies, or *Police Squad*, which parodies cop shows.

WIT

Wordplay. Consider these only slightly used examples. (All right, some are antiques.)

- I went to the cinema the other day and the sign said, "Adults: $7.00, Children: $3.50. So I checked my wallet and said, "Give me two boys and a girl."

- I went to a bookstore and asked the salesclerk, "Where's the self-help section?" She said if she told me, it would defeat the purpose.

- If you plan on giving someone unsolicited advice, always walk a mile in their shoes. That way they'll be barefoot and way behind you when they come after you.

How many of you believe in telekinesis? Raise my hand.

BON MOTS

Droll, often dry, this elegant wit often disguises wisdom.

- Depression is merely anger without the enthusiasm.

- A conclusion is the place where you got tired of thinking.

- Two wrongs . . . are only a beginning.

With so many ways to laugh, surely you can find a blanket of humor to wrap yourself in when you need to warm up after a cold spell. Clip cartoons and stick them where you'll see them. Keep a joke file. Practice finding the humor in everyday life. It's there, believe me.

Get Juicy

Keep a "Gratitude Journal." Every night, for at least a week, write five things about your day for which you're grateful. These can be large (my funny, loving son) or small (the toilet didn't plug today). Serious (I discovered a soul truth) or frivolous (the jingle bells sewn into my skirt made me smile every time I moved). Repeat the process for another week. And another, until gratitude becomes second nature. Gratitude for not having a toothache. Gratitude for simple miracles. There's nothing like a little thankfulness to lighten you and move you through blocks.

Get Juicy

This exercise works if you're feeling funky and dry or you want to write a humorous piece and can't seem to get in the swing. Laugh. Just that. Laugh. Largely. Keep laughing until you mean it—and you will.

Get Juicy

We tend to take ourselves way too seriously, which can get in the way of some interesting writing. How many times have you stopped yourself from writing something because it could be personally embarrassing? You're missing some rich stuff. This exercise will re-cast your most embarrassing moment by putting the distance of humor between you and your feelings of humiliation.

Sit or lie comfortably, arms and legs uncrossed. Follow your breath. No effort, just follow it. Starting with the top of your head and moving down, inventory each muscle group for tension on the in-breath, then release any you find on the out-breath. Repeat several breath cycles for each muscle group. Your forehead, face, and down the back of your head; your neck and shoulders; your arms and hands; your chest; your upper back; mid-back; abdomen; lower back and buttocks, your pelvis; your legs and feet. When you've reached your toes, make one last inventory to determine if any residual tension is hiding out. If you discover some, breathe into it until it relaxes.

Follow your breathing again and notice if it's slowed or deepened, if your back has relaxed into the floor or chair.

In this relaxed state, allow yourself to recall a highly embarrassing moment. Fully experience it. Who was there? What were they wearing. What were you wearing? Where were you? What smells were present? Sounds? Colors? Textures? What actually happened?

Now, step back. View it through a lens of humor. Leaven it, treat it as a funny story. You're in charge here; maybe you can't rewrite the facts of your history, but you most certainly can rewrite your response, can recast it as amusing rather than shaming. It may help to view it as a third person might, make yourself a character in a scene. Exaggerate the scene to hysterical proportions.

When you've fully experienced the new, lightened-up version, come back to the present, pull out your journal and write about it. Who knows? This might be the very scene you need for comic relief in your next novel.

Get Juicy

Surround yourself with things that make you laugh—the obvious, like funny books and movies, Gary Larsen date books and Dave Barry columns, but also the less obvious, like weird objects that make you grin. I know a guy who cultivated the humor habit in his decorating. It started in his yard. A sign announced "Warning: this property protected by guard turkey." But here's what's really funny about that. He honest-to-God had a guard turkey that would run gobbling at anyone who tried to enter. Beside his front door a dead tree's truncated branches sported a bevy of mismatched gloves. A dummy dressed in farmer flannel leaned out an upstairs window. A huge, stuffed sailfish draped with white twinkle lights graced the kitchen wall. You get the picture. You couldn't visit this guy's place and not laugh.

Ways to Use Humor

Humor can be wielded in several ways. It can be used as a sword to cut someone down. It can be used as a shield to hide behind. It can be used as a bridge to connect.

Humor used as a sword is classic put-down humor—Don Rickles, Phyllis Diller, Andrew Dice Clay. "Support bacteria. It's the only culture you'll ever have." "The problem with your gene pool is there's no life guard." It's humor that's used to control; and, while it can be funny to those hearing it, it draws uneasy laughter because it's definitely not funny to the butt of the joke.

Shield humor is self-deprecating, as in "I'll make fun of myself before you can." Sometimes, when fairly gentle, these can be funny, for example:

- I have an inferiority complex . . . but it's not a very good one.

- When I die, I'm leaving my body to science . . . fiction.

- I was trying to daydream, but my mind kept drifting.

- My mind is like a steel trap—rusty and illegal in thirty-seven states.

Shield humor can also be pretty painful, like the fat kid who says with a blush, "Hey, I'm so fat, when I sit around the house, I sit AROUND the house," or the skinny guy who says with a forced laugh, "I'm so thin, I have to run around in the shower to get wet." Ouch.

Finally, humor can be used as a bridge, as a way to connect to one another. Think of your favorite heroes. Chances are they employ humor as a bridge. This type of humor is often silly and, like all types of humor, always has an unexpected twist, but it includes rather than excludes. Bridge humor asks the important questions like:

- What ever happened to Preparations A through G?

- How much deeper would the ocean be without sponges?

- What's another word for "thesaurus?"

Humor enhances your writing and can move you through writer's block. It also illuminates character.

Creating Character Down to the Ground

Inevitably, a writer must write as a character, a believable, authentic character. Don't think you get out of it because you write nonfiction. Even if you write in your own voice, you are writing as a character—your own. Additionally, the best nonfiction tells a story and every story has characters. A story about working dogs will probably have a graph or two from a dog owner's perspective. That character needs to come off authentically for the story to bear weight.

Delving into character also serves the salutary function of letting your imagination out to dance. Naked. Shaking a tambourine. You can become anyone you want to be, tell that person's story. Stroll a mile in their loafers. Who needs reincarnation when you're a writer? We live hundreds of lives, thousands if we're prolific.

Character Types

Hero, heroine, villain, comic characters like sidekick confidantes or buffoon bad guys—every story-telling culture has its character types. It's easy to slide into predictability: white hat, black hat, and absolutely imperative that you don't if you're going to write authentically. Must characters serve a literary function, be in a story for a reason? Yep. Does that mean they can therefore be two-dimensional? Bite your tongue!

Every character isn't going to be fully developed. If your plot calls for a filling station attendant who provides a single necessary piece of information, we don't care where he went to Sunday school and that he doesn't phone his mother. Too much information is distracting and mistakenly signals the reader the character holds more import than he actually does. Provide a telling detail or two and move on.

But as for your protagonist (hero), antagonist (villain), and main supporting characters—you'll want to know where these people live, who they are. Generally, a protagonist is going to be likeable. Quirky, maybe, but not too. That's for the comic character sidekick. He'll face a series of obstacles and learn something in overcoming them. The antagonist is going to be sufficiently complex that we understand why he does the rotten things he does. The comic characters will provide comic relief and serve other functions like providing offbeat wisdom and filling in expositional gaps, that information the reader needs to know that isn't actually part of the story.

As an actor, I was bound by the confines of the script and what I could reasonably infer from it in creating character. A nonfiction writer is bound by reality. A fiction writer, however, is bound only by the permeable limits of authenticity.

The human psyche is a wondrous maelstrom of divine contradictions, yet there is a unique through-line to every character, however much it may be framed in swirling rococo dips and detours. How we find that through-line, that ground of being, becomes our work as writers.

Every person, fictional or otherwise, is a feast. As a writer, you need to know your character from soup to nuts. Typically, authors, like actors, ask themselves a series of questions to create a character study. Where did this character grow up? Family and educational background? Appearance? Marital status? Psychosocial make-up? These questions are helpful, immensely so, but I would suggest it helps to know a few basics before answering, "What does my hero dream about?"

For years debate has raged about whether nature or nurture—genes or environment—most influences human character and behavior. Any parent with more than one child will tell you each human being is unique before ever drawing breath. Even in the womb, a kid will show his stripes. Behavior may change dramatically, but always in a trajectory unique to that individual. My boy was a tough, colicky baby who became a sweet kid. But never in ways I expected.

Research suggests our genetic make-up is far more complex and determinative than we suspected. Studies of twins who were raised apart in wildly different environments show astonishing similarities in character and life paths, right down to the names of their spouses, in some cases. It's still too soon to call the fight, but the judges seem to be leaning on the side of "born with it."

This isn't to say free will is illusory. If I'd gone the way of my alcoholic genes, I'd be in the gutter or pushing daisies. Genetic predispositions can be overcome. Let's hear it for Prozac. Or 12-step programs, prayer, hypnosis, or whatever change agent works for you. And for your character. What's important is that you decide your character's basic make-up, then extrapolate from there. Try on the following infrastructures so your character has a thoroughfare to move around on rather than flailing through the wilderness.

Worldview

Ask whether your character is essentially an optimist or at core a pessimist. Maybe we're born with exuberance or despair as a defining trait. Perhaps events from our childhood shape our view. We may even serve as unwitting psychic containers for the unconscious projections of others, sort of a "sins of the fathers" theory. Whatever the case, a character's basic outlook figures large in how she deals with life.

In World War II concentration camps, Victor Frankl observed that while some people died quickly when confronted with the monstrous conditions of the camps, others were able to embrace their suffering and find meaning in it. Those who found meaning survived.

Attitude is everything. Worldview won't necessarily predetermine character and behavior, but will unquestionably color the hows and whys of a life. If a character comes from the belief that the world is essentially a loving place, he will be shaped differently, in myriad ways both large and small, than a character who comes from fear.

Health and Appearance

Consider health problems that might arise from a constricted worldview: hypertension, colitis, ulcers, migraines, TMJ. On the other hand, an optimistic, jump-right-in attitude may engender accidents. Optimism doesn't necessarily equate with impulsiveness, but it could.

Think about how worldview influences your character's appearance. For example, appearance may be something an optimist doesn't think about because it doesn't matter, or it may mean bright, skintight, younger-than-her years clothing because any day now she's going to drop that ten pounds and look thirty again. Avoiding colors and dressing in shades of gray are obvious choices for a pessimist, but perhaps there are more subtle indications of a mistrustful attitude, like baggy clothes that hide the body or painful body piercing.

Psychological Profile

Worldview will influence how tightly beliefs are held. Coming from fear tends to create reactive stridency in beliefs, whatever they may be, while coming from love could make a person so tolerant as to become wishy-washy. Basic worldview may alter a character's need for control. A fearful person has a greater need to feel in control, which could manifest in interesting ways: scheduling down to the gnat's tushie, constantly "checking-in," saying one thing while doing another, and other passive-aggressive behaviors.

I touched earlier on the notion of unconscious projections onto others. This is tricky, fascinating stuff. A character may have an emotional issue passed on through a parent that doesn't actually belong to him yet influences his behavior until he's able to bring it to consciousness and release it. For this very reason, the Buddhist tradition of cleaning one's karma isn't simply for the self, but for all generations that have been or are yet to come.

Unconscious projection can also work on a temporary, stranger-to-stranger level. A dear friend of mine who is a therapist once interviewed a woman who had attempted suicide ten years before by setting herself on fire. During the interview, my friend, normally the soul of compassion, felt uncontrollable antagonism toward the woman, even sadistic, bullying feelings. He wanted to yell at her, "So you wanted to commit suicide, huh? Well, you didn't do a very good job of it!" His thoughts scared him; he couldn't understand where they had come from.

During the course of their interview, my friend learned that the woman had been savaged by her father all her life. Indeed, her original intent at the time she set herself on fire had been to first torture and kill her father, then kill herself. It took my friend a long time to understand his reaction to this woman. She had projected her unconscious onto my friend; my friend had become her father, complete with sadistic feelings.

If you have a character who is hypersensitive to others' emotional content, even their unspoken content, be aware of what that means in behavioral terms. I've known "empaths" who actually experienced other people's physical or emotional pain. Like chameleons, when they were removed from painful situations, what appeared to be pessimism lifted. Maybe that crazy hermit lives out there for a reason; she can't take the pain. When confronted with a social situation, she may react both compassionately and irrationally, first feeling the pain, then flinging herself from it.

Don't make the mistake of writing all villains as pessimists who come from fear and all heroes as optimists who come from love. Mix it up to create a more interesting story. What about a saint-in-training whose overweening compassion and belief in diversity allow skinheads to infiltrate a neighborhood unchecked, or a genuine son of a bitch whose strict moral code saves the day. What if the saint-in-training was a pessimist? Now we're getting interesting. I know plenty of pessimists who are fine people; but their worldviews do affect who and how they are.

Get Juicy

Decide if your protagonist comes from love or fear, believes the world is basically a good place or not to be trusted. Once you've determined an optimistic or pessimistic worldview, answer the following questions about the character.

• Health and Appearance

_____

_____

_____

_____

_____

• Psychological profile

Beliefs

_____

_____

_____

_____

On a scale of 1 to 10, with 10 being absolute rigidity, how tightly are these beliefs held?

_____

Need for control: On a scale of 1 to 10, with 10 being the consummate control freak, where does your character land in needing to control his environment?

_____

How is this manifested?

_____

_____

_____

- Emotional sensitivity/empathy

Does the character "feel your pain" and his own or is he able to compartmentalize?

_____

_____

_____

What unconscious projections operate in this character's life?

_____

_____

_____

_____

Given the previous responses, fill in the following:

- Occupation:

  _____

- Educational background:

  _____

- Marital history:

  _____

- Family background:

  _____

  _____

  _____

- Personality type:

  Intelligence level:

  _____

  Values:

  _____

  _____

  Spiritual beliefs:

  _____

  _____

Self-esteem:

_____

Body image:

_____

Greatest desire:

_____

Greatest obstacle to that desire:

_____

Learning Style

How your character learns determines in large part how she sees/hears/feels the world. An auditory learner will construct the world and order priorities differently than a visual learner. The former may have a home filled with music and high-tech equipment, probably loves to talk on the phone. The latter may have a slew of post-its on his fridge and images on the walls, even if they're torn from a magazine and pasted up in a rough wood shack.

Alice Walker uses a lovely character trait in _The Color Purple_. She has her protagonist constantly chewing something—a rubber band, a leaf, a slip of fabric. Aside from the metaphoric value of eating life's tiniest details, this clear kinesthetic tendency shows a lot about the character. Celie is a strong kinesthetic, for whom sensuality matters deeply, as much as she has to suppress it. This grounds her, makes her earthy and immediate.

Get Juicy

Choose a primary learning style for your character. Now, choose a secondary. Finally, choose one that's weak. You may stay with the big three: auditory, visual or kinesthetic. Or you may wish to expand into the various learning styles posited by Howard Gardner:

- musical

- bodily-kinesthetic

- logical-mathematical

- linguistic

- spatial

- interpersonal

- intrapersonal

- naturalist

Primary Learning Style:

_____

Secondary Learning Style:

_____

Weak on:

_____

With this information, describe your character's:

Habitat: _____

_____

_____

Favorite Activities: _____

_____

_____

Occupation: _____

_____

_____

Goals/dreams: _____

_____

_____

Sense of Humor

Your characters' senses of humor say a lot about them. If Uncle Fred guffaws at the Three Stooges and Aunt Ethel titters at droll bon mots, you've mined major character distinctions with few words. Not just what type, but how your characters use humor is illustrative.

Sword humor would be a good pick for an angry, controlling character. The abusive father who verbally roughs up his son, then laughs and asks, "Can't you take a joke?" The jealous girlfriend who makes a point of laughing about her boyfriend's expansive gut in front of dinner guests.

Shield humor broadcasts a self-effacing or insecure character, the plain Jane who hides her pain behind a barrage of one-liners, the physically challenged teen who cracks "crip" jokes. Used gently, shield humor telegraphs a Jimmy Stewart "just folks" kinda guy. Wielded forcefully, it suggests a full-blown neurotic trying to cover.

Bridge humor is the kind that asks, "Do you think when they asked George Washington for ID he just whipped out a quarter?" Because this humor hurts no one and lets everybody laugh, it's a good choice for a well-adjusted character or maybe one who just wants everybody to be happy. (Not to be confused with a "No, no, I'll just sit here in the dark" co-dependent, who would probably go with subtle put-down or shield as methods of control.)

Perhaps the most chilling character imaginable is one with no sense of humor at all. Makes me cold just thinking about it.

Get Juicy

Create a character based on the following types and uses of humor.

Slapstick/Sword:

● Name:

_____

● Age:

_____

- Gender:

  _____

- Appearance:

  _____

  _____

- Occupation:

  _____

  _____

- Intelligence level/educational background:

  _____

  _____

- Marital history:

  _____

  _____

- Family background: (Ethnicity, pets, socioeconomic background, dynamics)

  _____

  _____

  _____

  _____

- Personality type:

  _____

  _____

  Extrovert/introvert:

  _____

  Self-esteem:

  _____

  _____

  Worldview:

  _____

  _____

  Body image:

  _____

  _____

- Spiritual beliefs:

  _____

  _____

- Where does this character live?

  _____

  _____

- Greatest desire:

  _____

  _____

- Greatest obstacle to that desire:

  _____

  _____

Wit/Shield:

- Name:

  _____

- Age:

  _____

- Gender:

  _____

- Appearance:

  _____

  _____

- Occupation:

  _____

  _____

  _____

- Intelligence level/educational background:

  _____

  _____

- Marital history:

  _____

  _____

- Family background: (Ethnicity, pets, socioeconomic background, dynamics)

  _____

  _____

- Personality type:

  _____

  _____

  Extrovert/introvert:

  _____

  Self-esteem:

  _____

  _____

  Worldview:

  _____

  _____

Body image:

_____

_____

● Spiritual beliefs:

_____

_____

● Where does this character live?

_____

_____

● Greatest desire:

_____

_____

● Greatest obstacle to that desire:

_____

_____

If you're feeling scrappy, take these characters and put them into a humorous scene. Go a little crazy, nobody's watching. People working in a whipped-cream factory (a messier version of Lucy and Ethel in the candy factory), two sodbusters set loose in the big city, a New York fashion maven dropped on an unsuspecting small Indiana town. What strikes you as funny?

Humor is probably the toughest genre to write, so don't worry if your initial foray in shaping a comic scene feels like a block of wood and you're a stick of butter. Just explore and get a little grease slopped around.

It will be tempting to exaggerate comic characters and that's perfectly appropriate. Humor relies on exaggeration. But this doesn't mean the character becomes a cartoon or is inauthentic. The best comedy arises from characters who are three-dimensional and absolutely true to themselves. Think Lucille Ball's character in *I Love Lucy*. Over-the-top exaggerated? Absolutely. True to herself? You bet.

Centers of Gravity

In my years as an actor and acting teacher, I found the most crucial fact about any character was the person's center of gravity. I once played Elmire in Moliere's *Tartuffe*, an ultra-sophisticated and mannered play from the French Renaissance. I went quite literally from performing in that show to overlapping rehearsals for the nurse in Shakespeare's *Romeo and Juliet*. The nurse is a bawdy, lower class English wench; Elmire, a delicate, upper class French lady. I'm a method actor, meaning I come from the emotional truth of a character. Oy.

What saved my bacon then and throughout my acting days was finding each character's center of gravity. Elmire came from her chest—high and proud. Everything else fell into place: voice, gestures, manner, walk, personality. The nurse came from her gut—blowzy, coarse, and ribald.

Get Juicy

Begin moving around the room normally. Then, shift to moving from your chest. Experience what that feels like, how it affects the rest of your body. How it affects your attitude and feelings. Walk from your chest for at least three minutes, until you fully get what that's like. Try a few words. If you find yourself tongue-tied, use this phrase an old actor I used to work with said whenever she forgot her lines—even if the play was Shakespeare—"My uncle drives a gold Cadillac, you know."

Now switch to leading from your gut. Notice the differences. Try a few words. Your uncle driving a gold Cadillac may take on a whole new meaning.

When you're ready, switch to leading from your knees. From your crotch. From your forehead. From your chin. Play with each character; fully explore the implications of each center of gravity.

Now, write about the experience. Draft a character study for each center of gravity, assigning a name, physical life, psycho/emotional life, and social information like education, class and family background. What does each want more than anything? If you get stuck, get up and do the center you're working on again until the character becomes clear to you.

Chest Center of Gravity

- Physical life: (appearance, identifying traits, self-image)

_____

_____

- Psycho/emotional life: (personality, spiritual beliefs, intelligence)

  _____

  _____

- Social information: (ethnicity, family background, economic class, education, marital history)

  _____

  _____

- Greatest desire?

  _____

  _____

- Deepest fear?

  _____

  _____

Repeat this exercise for centers of gravity from:

- Gut

- Knees

- Crotch

- Forehead

- Chin

Centers of gravity work best for kinesthetic learners, though I've found them helpful for all types of learners.

Create Your Own Infrastructures

Maybe you know Meyers-Briggs personality profiles, or Ennegram personality types. Maybe you're up on astrological signs or Ayurvedic physical/emotional types or Maslow's Hierarchy of Needs. Whatever defining paradigm you find to be true works as a skeleton from which you can flesh your characters. Get to the library and try on a few coats; see what fits.

Personality Traits

Why should the psychologists or the ancient Egyptians have all the fun? Using a paradigm that interests you or one you've made up out of whole cloth (does anybody really know what makes humans tick?), try the exercise below to create a personality type.

Get Juicy

Circle ten traits from the following list. These traits may be notoriously random, assuming the shrinks or the stars or the Egyptians don't really know any more than we do about human behavior, or carefully analytic, assuming they do. Based on those traits, create a character.

powerful	shy	friendly	melancholy
trite	boastful	lazy	giddy
athletic	sensitive	sexy	insecure
intellectual	strange	perfect	clumsy
funny	trusting	angry	withdrawn
superficial	elegant	serious	shallow
sneaky	hidden	proud	fierce
cute	hedonistic	loud	phony
truthful	weak	fussy	conceited
delicate	tricky	limited	soft
intelligent	vulgar	cruel	optimistic
deep	beautiful	instinctive	homely
rural	varied	amorous	creative
good	playful	religious	energetic
lost	negative	vivacious	fragile
frantic	generous	moody	picky
tentative	aggressive	zany	boastful
educated	handy	lusty	businesslike
jealous	puny	evil	suspicious
angry	careful	loving	motherly

masculine	quick	brilliant	demanding
bubbly	spiritual	authentic	mean
daft	thrifty	nasty	guarded
frenetic	macho	beastly	extravagant
superior	scary	frightened	sensual
dirty	frail	emotional	sexual
passive	dedicated	cheap	composed
brave	strong	precise	unusual
firm	feminine	centered	grim
humorous	smart	slow	lawful
controlled	thoughtful	empathic	stupid
proper	stuffy	cowardly	devious
manipulative	manic	reckless	scattered
fearful	timid	snappy	wicked
cynical	wild	sloppy	haughty
carefree	loyal	respectful	respectable
moral	charismatic	amoral	rigid
flexible	exuberant	vulnerable	conventional
wacky	wise	wistful	whimsical

Based on these traits, write a character study:

- Physical life (appearance, identifying traits, self-image):

  _____

  _____

  _____

- Psycho/emotional life (personality, spiritual beliefs, intelligence):

  _____

  _____

  _____

  _____

- Social information (ethnicity, family background, marital status, economic class, education):

  _____

  _____

  _____

- Greatest desire?

  _____

  _____

- Deepest fear?

_____

_____

Now, circle ten more in a different color of ink and create another character.

It's All About the Ears

Thought I forgot about you auditory learners? Not a chance. You get your very own earfrastructure.

Get Juicy

Remember the voice types you collected back in week two? Pick the two or three most interesting and create characters based solely on how they sound. Avoid people you know well, as prior knowledge of personality will corrupt the exercise. Go strictly with the voice. The person may have weighed ninety pounds and been seventy-eight years old, but if the voice was a booming bass, go with the booming bass and all it implies. Want to try stretching your auditory limits? Create a sound portrait of the person using auditory cues as personality traits. For example, a tinny, rattling character is very different than a hushed, mellifluous one.

Description of voice: _____

Character Study:

- Physical life: (appearance, identifying traits, self-image)

_____

_____

_____

_____

- Psycho/emotional life: (personality, spiritual beliefs, intelligence)

_____

_____

_____

- Social information: (ethnicity, family background, economic class, education)

_____

_____

_____

- Greatest desire?

_____

_____

- Deepest fear?

_____

_____

_____

The Fool

This character is too fun not to try. The fool is a classic comic character—the way-off-center weirdo who speaks crazy wisdom. In certain Native American tribes, a "menashe" used sarcasm and backward foolishness to show tribal members the error of their ways or simply to get them to keep an open mind. If someone brought back blankets from the Army that were suspected of being contaminated with smallpox, the menashe would trail the person and loudly "admire" the acquisition. Or he would ride into camp backward, leap off his pony and, with his back to the tribe, greet them by saying "Good-bye." Keep an open mind.

Behind the fool's foolishness lies wisdom. And more than a little pain. The mix of dark and light is what makes the fool—or any character—compelling. Consider the following fools, then sketch out one of your own.

Lily Tomlin's wise fool, Trudy, in *Search for Signs of Intelligent Life in the Universe*, has this take on conventional reality:

"I refuse to be intimidated by reality anymore. After all, what is reality anyway? Nothin' but a collective hunch. My space chums think reality was once a primitive method of crowd control that got out of hand . . . I made some studies, and reality is the leading cause of stress among those in touch with it. I can take it in small doses, but as a lifestyle I found it too confining. It was just too needful— it expected me to be there for it *all* the time, and with all I have to do, I had to let something go. Now, since I put reality on the back burner, my days are jam-packed and fun-filled."

In the following piece, consider what types of humor this wise fool employs.

Ciel, from the play *Earth People Looking at Sky*

> *Ciel lives on the streets. She comes from deep in her gut, locus of pain and glory. She emits a guttural "hmmm" from the back of her throat almost constantly and smacks her lips as if thirsty, the result, perhaps, of her medication. She shuffles along hunched over, eyes piercing left and right, distrustful, seeking.*
>
> *She is a powerfully built woman; the layers of shapeless clothes she wears make her appear even larger, although years of living on the streets have taken their toll in her face and on her shuffling gait. She wears a raggedy photographer's vest, and a wild array of found objects adorn its many pockets: one badge, "Tawanda," another, "Whales Save Us;" a string of African trade beads looped between two pockets; a chipped porcelain pin in pink ceramic of two women dancing; a bent Brownie pin; a multitude of brightly colored scarves. Clothespins, any number of clothespins, march across her chest like a guerrilla's bandoleer.*
>
> *There are clothespins on her hat, too, arranged in a curving row along the brim of an Australian-buttoned slouch, once beige but now the color of overused dishwater. As Ciel walks briskly to the edge of the stage her lips pouch in and out, in and out, accompanied by a soft, nasal "hmmm," "hmmm," "hmmm." She stops at the edge of the stage and stares out at the audience. She speaks.*

"I WON'T WORK FOR FOOD. NOOOOO WAY! I WILL <u>NOT</u> WORK FOR ANY DAMN FOOD. Shoo. How do I know if you can even cook? Work for food, my butt. I'll get my sorry ass down to the mission. Thursday is mac 'n' cheese day. I do love how they do that mac 'n' cheese. Father Jim opens a mean package.

"I been on the streets forever, child, since you were a pup in your daddy's knee-high eye. I'm as old as the oldest jackrabbit and as new as the button on a Christmas pony. But I ain't no bag lady, you hear me? I am a 'habitat-challenged consumer recycler'. *(Ciel cackles hysterically, then abruptly stops and points to an audience member.)*

"You don't think that you know me; but you do child, you do.

"I been living over behind the new Safeway. Betty and her two kids live back there too. Coupla nice kids, Betty's got. We found us an almost full deck of playing cards one time. Says 'United' on them cards. I like that. United. Beats the alternative.

"We filled in the missing cards with some cardboard that wasn't too munged outta the dumpster. We get a lot of use out of those cards, though I got to admit it kinda takes the surprise out of it when you see one of them munged cardboard cards come flappin' down. I do my best not to know it's either the eight of spades or the queen of hearts.

"That Safeway, it's a nicer neighborhood, child, very upscale, very uptown. They got sushi in their dumpster. You see my mouth movin'? I be chewing sushi in my sleep.

"Don't think I ever sleep, child. I never sleep. I am awake to all humanity, awake for all humanity. Oh, I know what you're thinking—people who live on the streets want to be there. What you been snortin'? I am the exception that rules the proof. Nobody of sound mind wants to live on these nasty old streets. Me, I gotta motion mind, not a sound one. But Betty, she's as sound as a dollar. You think she wants to live by some old dumpster behind the Safeway? You ever smell week-old sushi? Takes all the shi-shi out of it.

"But as for me . . . you think I have to be on the streets? *(she snorts)* My grandmother owned half of Boise, child, no way this old girl has to live on any street. I could be reclining in my La-Z-Boy watching Vanna spin those letters on my big screen, if I had a mind to. But I live out here as a sacrifice for my species. I live out here to spare and protect YOU, child.

"Lemme tell you something. When things got bad for the Lakota people, several men from the tribe would make a Sun Dance. You know that Sun Dance, child? Well, I didn't think you would. What do you modern, tribeless people know about sacrifice?

"These Lakota men would whittle bone and pierce their chests with it, then attach rawhide thongs to those pieces of bone. Then, those rawhide ropes would be drawn up so those men would be lifted off the ground by their chests, slowly twirling in exquisite anguish. They'd whistle on sacred bone flutes as they dangled. For days, child. Days. No food, no water, no sleep. Only dancing with death for the good of their people.

"Two winters ago, I took me a ice pick I happened upon in The Home Depot. I put that thing in flame – sterilized it and made it holy. Then I called down all my spirit guides and in my finest moment, I pierced my chest—just here.

"While the blood trickled down, I danced. *(She begins to dance a shuffling stomp dance, bathed in the glow of blood-red spotlights.)*

"I danced for the spring to come. I danced for life to continue on this crazed and grieving planet. *(She dances. Takes out whistle and whistles while dancing)*

"Isn't this a fine whistle? It's not made outta bone. It's a contemporary sacred whistle. Made outta <u>plastic</u>. I found it in the dumpster. Isn't it amazing what people throw away?

(She dances and whistles, as a drum starts to pound a slow, heavy heartbeat.)

"But as I danced, child, I had a revelation and it stopped me right in the middle of a spin. *(She stops abruptly)* I was missin' it, child. I was arrogant thinkin' my pain alone gonna spare somebody. Maybe we'll find our own meaning in our pain, but can't nobody stop somebody else's pain with their own.

"I didn't understand the real nature of sacrifice.

"Sacrifice is sloggin' through every day with your eyes turned out. Sacrifice is mutterin' a prayer when you'd just as 'lief curse. And if you do it right, sacrifice can feel like sacrament. Really do it right and sacrifice feels like celebration.

(Resumes dancing) "So I live out here as a prayer for you people. I got my spirit guides to protect me. *(Listens to voices only she can hear)* "Nah, now, you don't need to be introduced to these folks. *(Listens intently)* You feel my mind movin'? I said 'NO.' *(Looks at audience member)* You think I'm crazy, don't you?

"Maybe you're right.

"Maybe you're wrong.

"But I'll tell you something. You let Betty and her two kids make the sacrifice for you now, someday you gonna have to dance the Sun Dance." *(Slowly dances, whistling)*

Get Juicy

Paint a word portrait of your own fool. Maybe your fool has wisdom. Maybe not. But she'll never be accused of striking up the bland. Your character may be a wizened old cracker instead of a street person, or an idiot savant who plays Rachmaninoff, or your great aunt who kept a dead cricket collection and made you spice cake as she dealt out scrambled advice you're still living by. Or maybe a seven-year-old Britney Spears wanna-be. Dip your foot into the fool's water and see what washes.

Describe your fool:

_____

_____

_____

_____

_____

_____

_____

_____

_____

Here comes the fun part. Now that you've got this fool where you want her, consider spending at least part of a day in character.

If your character is a boot-scootin' flirt with big hair and vermilion lips, and you're the essence of reserve, what a great opportunity you've created for yourself! Don't cheat and go back to re-dignify a wild and crazy character. Go with it.

I once spent a morning at a busy farmer's market as a loopy, Yenta-ish, homeless woman. I was playing the character in a show and, as a kinesthetic learner, needed to "get" her in an experiential way. It was a revelation. Actors do this all the time to understand their characters. Why should they have all the fun?

After spending time as your character, find a quiet corner, pull out your journal and write about the experience. Who knows? It may sail you in a completely unexpected direction.

Knowing What to Write About

Life Themes and Insights

Knowing what you want to write about is half the battle. Instead of "write what you know," I'd advise "write what you care about." Writing fueled by passion is vivid, immediate, deeply present. Yet, instead of writing from our hearts, many of us still write from the high altar of "should." A lot of us wouldn't be able to say what we want to write about if it came up and kissed us. With a pinch on the fanny.

Free journaling will help. Filling in this self-discovery chart will, too.

Get Juicy

Claudia Johnson, a wonderful film teacher in Florida, suggests her students fill out what she calls, "Le Menu." I've adapted her ideas, as follows. This is also a great tool for discovering your characters' inner lives.

Self Discovery Chart

What I Love:

Stephen Daniel Jones, river rocks, polished rocks, Gilad's workouts, hashbrown-casserole, History Channel,

What I Hate:

Racism, Sexism,

What Comforts Me:

music (gospel, soul, R&B, Jazz,)
Silence,

Who Loves Me:
Stephen Daniel Jones, and many more...

What I Dream:

_____

_____

_____

_____

_____

What I Fear:

_____

_____

_____

_____

_____

What I Believe:

_____

_____

_____

_____

_____

What I Value:

_____

_____

_____

_____

_____

What I Want:

_____

_____

_____

_____

_____

What I Know About:

_____

_____

_____

_____

_____

People Who Have Made a Difference in My Life:

_____

_____

_____

_____

_____

_____

Discoveries and Decisions That Have Made a Difference in My Life:

_____

_____

_____

_____

_____

_____

Update this little chart on a regular basis. If you're stuck for what to write, review it. Maybe you're trying to write about things that don't matter to you, an open invitation to literary quagmire.

Mind you, I admit that if you're being paid by the word, you can care about a lot of stuff. But face it, the real stuff is the good stuff is the real stuff. (Thank you Gertrude Stein.)

Still not sure what to write about?

Authenticity

Go there. In any way you can. Authenticity is the source of our creative truth, what we need to be writing about. You may be writing a screwball comedy, but if you're writing from your center, it will ring truer and, so, be funnier.

But how do you find your center when you've been living on the fringe? Too many of us have lived someone else's life for all of ours—the life our mother wanted, or our husband, or our seventh-grade teacher, or the media. Sorting our own truth from deeply internalized conditioning can feel like a hard freeze in winter, can make Jason's search for the golden fleece look like a stroll in the country, but it can be done. Meditation helps. Therapy helps. Creating helps.

Take this completely arbitrary self-knowledge test. There will be no quiz later, but maybe it will get you mulling about what matters to you. Then, maybe it will show up in your free-journal.

Totally Arbitrary Self-Knowledge Quiz

1. If your house caught fire, what one thing (not person) would you save? Why?

   _____

   _____

_____

_____

_____

_____

2. For what (and whom) are you grateful? Why?

_____

_____

_____

_____

_____

_____

3. What (and whom) do you resent? Why?

_____

_____

_____

_____

_____

_____

4. How do you define love? List examples.

_____

_____

_____

_____

_____

_____

5. You had a disturbing dream. What was it?

_____

_____

_____

_____

_____

6. When you were a child, you had a secret desire. What was it?

_____

_____

_____

_____

_____

7. What were your two most embarrassing moments?

_____

_____

_____

_____

_____

8. What were your two proudest moments?

_____

_____

_____

_____

_____

9. If you could live five other lives, whose would they be? Why?

_____

_____

_____

_____

_____

10. Would you rather die by ice or fire? Why?

_____

_____

_____

_____

_____

11. What is your ideal animal? Why?

_____

_____

_____

_____

_____

12. What is your ideal car? Why?

_____

_____

_____

_____

_____

13. Do you have a notion of the Divine? What is it?

_____

_____

_____

_____

_____

_____

14. Where and how do you experience wonder?

_____

_____

_____

_____

_____

By now, you should be getting a good idea of what matters to you. Let's find out more.

Get Juicy

This exercise hails from the '70s and '80s humanistic psychology movement and still holds water. In your journal, number along the left side of a fresh page "1" through "100" on every other line. Be sure to leave space below each number. Start each sentence with, "I want . . ." Then, fill in the blanks with everything you want, from the least to the greatest. Maybe you want fresh strawberries. A new Eurovan. A trip to the Rockies. A counseling degree. A yurt in Northern New Mexico. Put it all down, in great specificity, the real and the fantastic. To be twenty again. Heck, to be thirty again.

You may need to take some time with this, especially if you're used to putting off your own wants for the sake of the family. Consider what you want in your life in these areas: Spirituality, Creativity, Home, Adventure & Recreation, Livelihood/Career, Health, Friends and Family, Material Goods. Write them down. In gnat's-tushie detail.

I want _____

_____

I want _____

_____

I want _____

_____

I want _____

_____

I want _____

_____

I want _____

_____

I want _____

_____

I want _____

_____

I want _____

_____

I want _____

_____

I want _____

_____

I want _____

_____

Keep going 'til you're all wanted out.

When you've completed this section of the exercise, you'll have a good sense of what you want. At least on the apparent level.

Now, go back over your list to discover what you *really* want. Write on the blank line you left underneath each item how you would feel if you received what you wrote. What does each item represent for you? This may take some onion-peeling, layer by layer. A Eurovan represents freedom to me. The Rockies: spirituality, unconstrained by others. That's what you *really* want. Peace of mind, joy, freedom. Find out what really matters. Those are themes you should be writing about.

Finally, ask yourself if what you originally thought you wanted is in fact the best way to get what you *really* want. If what you'd get from a book deal with Bantam is your mother's approval, maybe there's a better, or at least easier way of getting it (maybe you can give it to yourself). Sometimes, of course, a Eurovan is just a Eurovan and it's exactly what you want, symbol-shmimbol.

Get Juicy

This is another exercise that's been around forever. List twenty people you admire. Albert Schweitzer, Oprah Winfrey, your mother, your father. Whomever they may be, write them down. Next to each person's name, write a brief description of why you admire this person. Leonardo da Vinci for his multi-faceted talent; Amelia Earhart for her sense of adventure; Martin Luther King, Jr. for his dedication to an important cause; Julian of Norwich for her mystic understanding. What are yours?

When you have a list, review the descriptor words. Do certain themes keep coming up? Maybe you have a strong pull toward adventure that you never knew about. Or integrity, self-actualization, authenticity, ultimate style, zaniness. Recurring ideas are themes you should write about. They matter to you, and why in the world would you write about something that doesn't matter?

What do you like to read? Check the stack next to your bed. What appeals to you? Forget what you're supposed to like. My brother is a sociology professor who writes with perspicacity and depth about the noted semiotics philosopher, Jacques Derrida. I'm well educated. Do I enjoy reading about this most esteemed thinker? Spare me. I'd rather have a root canal. Without benefit of anesthetic.

What do you sneak to read when you go to the dentist's office? Where are you drawn when perusing a friend's library? What do you love to read? That's the genre you ought to be writing. Or at least trying. Maybe the rest of your family writes serious tomes that are published by prestigious European academic presses, like my family; but, hey, if bizarre love stories about connection are your real passion, so be it. Ain't running any race except with the authenticity clock.

Curiosity Invigorates the Cat

In *How to Think Like Leonardo*, Michael Gelb claims curiosity as the first and foremost of seven da Vincian principles. He says that requisite to being fully realized is "an insatiably curious approach to life and an unrelenting quest for continuous learning."

Get Juicy

In no particular order, list ten things you're curious about.

1. _____

2. _____

3. _____

4. _____

5. _____

6. _____

7. _____

8. _____

9. _____

10. _____

From your list, pick one subject to explore. This may mean spelunking a cave in Thailand or simply getting on the Net to learn how many cultivars of iris there are. Maybe you have an unspoken yen to learn more about mixed-race relationships during the Civil War or how the introduction of the thresher changed the complexion of 19th century farming. Pick one you can learn about experientially (I have the good fortune to live near a park with an underwater viewing area of a large population of manatees, for example) or one you'll explore strictly through archives and books. Once you've satisfied your curiosity, write about your new expertise.

Cultivate what's known in Zen as "beginner's mind," that openness to experience that a rank but avid beginner has. The curiosity of a new kitten. Of a two-year-old. Investigate everything. You may find you love something you never imagined you would. (Maybe even Derrida, but I doubt it.) Break through what Jane Wagoner calls the "confines of the appropriate."

Write a chapter of a steamy romance. A scene from a thriller. What puts you in the zone, oblivious to the passage of time and exhilarated at the end of a long day at the keyboard? Write that.

Creative Manifesto

Remember the Desiderata posters that were all the rage back in the 70s and the similar wall art diatribes since then, like the one based on the book *Everything I Ever Needed to Know I Learned in Kindergarten*? In this section you'll create your own philosophy poster of personal truths about your artistic process. Take time with this, let the truth come out on its own legs. Practice the "Going Down" exercise that follows and allow your creative truths to seep out as gently as soft rain. Or flare like fireworks over an Independence Day lake. But not slammed out with a sledgehammer.

Going Down

Establish a quiet, serene place in your home where you can plumb the depths on a regular basis, free of interruption. Turn off the phone ringer. Lock the door. Alert your family to give you space. In our home we have a "breathing room" dedicated to meditation and quiet. We figured that was more important than a separate dining room.

As you begin, ask for guidance about what you need to know to be a fully authentic creative artist. Then, don't think about it again.

Lie or sit quietly, arms at your sides, legs and feet uncrossed. Close your eyes. Settle. Notice your breath. Don't try to change it, simply notice it. Notice where it comes in at your nostrils, where it goes after that, down your throat, into your lungs, how it comes back out. Follow it for several minutes.

As your mind skitters about like a giddy puppy—and it will—gently return your focus to your breathing. Just let yourself be.

After several minutes, you'll probably notice your breathing has slowed and deepened. You may feel a calm center where before was fizz or clench. From this deep space, listen. Allow what you need to know to bubble up. Wait patiently. The answer may not come right then and it may come in a disguised form, but if you're awake to it, it will be there. Often right now in full Technicolor. Or a full Technicolor answer to yesterday's unresolved dilemma. The universe isn't terribly concerned about linear resolution.

If you're having trouble hearing what your psyche has to tell you, imagine yourself on a path. Visualize it in multi-sensory detail. Is there a breeze? What's the temperature? What is the environment in which you're walking—forest, beach, countryside, cityscape? You notice a figure in the distance coming toward you. With a great feeling of warmth and joy, you realize this is your muse, the inspiration for your creativity. This may be your personal notion of the divine, or something entirely different. It's whatever you deem your muse, that creative spirit within.

The figure comes closer, then stops. With deep love and wisdom, your muse tells you those truths you need to know and remember in your creative work.

When you've finished receiving this wisdom, gently bring yourself back to the room and open your eyes. Write down any insights in your journal. Repeat this process until it feels complete, then type up your truths in fonts you enjoy and print them out. You're ready for your Creative Manifesto.

Alternative Juice

If you're tired or put off by yet another guided visualization, mull this question in your journal this week: what do I need to know to realize my creative potential? Write that prompt at the top of the page and let your fingers fly to the answers without thinking or censoring.

Get Juicy

Buy a large sheet of poster board. From your image file or from magazines, pull pictures that appeal to you, that somehow speak to you as a creative being. Choose images that croon your true name, that in some way nourish your creative spirit. You may wish to include some images of your ideal future.

Cut and paste these images on the poster board in any way that appeals to you. Over or around the images, either write or paste typed or calligraphied truths. You may wish to add ribbons, pressed flowers, objects that have meaning for you. This is your Creative Manifesto. It is your statement to yourself and the world about what is important to you as a creative being. Give it a prominent place in your heart and on your wall near where you write.

I've had students who created luscious collages, rich in texture and detail. I've had students cover every square centimeter with images and text. I've had students who cut and pasted images in patterns, using negative space as a major design element. I had one student who spent an hour looking for images, found one and yelped in glee. Her Creative Manifesto consisted of a single picture of a laughing woman dressed in a mud-spattered wedding gown. Maggie, a poet, was working on her fifth marriage and possessed a great sense of humor. I suspect she also possessed a continually refreshed sense of optimism.

Alternatively, find a box or overnight case and create your own personal creativity altar. Cover the outside and inside with fabric, foil, feathers, buttons, badges, buffoonery—whatever strikes you as most true in an aesthetic sense. Include a scroll of your necessary truths.

Here's a sample Creative Manifesto. Feel free to take anything you find relevant.

- Respect yourself. Respect your creativity. Let it flow through you like sun through clear water.

- Trust the process, surrender the results.

- Get out of your own way.

- Speak your truth, with your mouth and with your hand, in your art and in your life. Speak your truth.

- Know you aren't alone.

- Take your power and use it wisely.

- Forgive those who would shame your creativity. Avoid them assiduously.

- Slow down.

- Turn to the earth. Walk her wild places. Crawl into nature's lap and let her stroke your hair.

- Spend time alone. Take quiet time every day.

- Rest when you need rest.

- Respect all living things, including yourself.

- Look at your anger. Let it lead you to action, not push you around.

- "Perseverance furthers."

- Take care of yourself. Take care of your sisters and brothers.

- Take a risk.

- Have fun.

- Back down your fears. Make them allies.

- Dance lightly with your ghosts.

- Ask for grace. Don't expect it, but lean back in it and let it wash over you when it comes.

- Open. Let creation work through you.

- Breathe. Deeply.

- Let yourself evolve.

- Be at ease. Watch the passing show with wonder, amusement and the occasional Bronx cheer.

- Show up. Learn the difference between necessary incubation and procrastination.

- Follow the energy. Resistance is worse than futile.

- Seek out warm, gutsy people living authentic lives. Be one.

- Feel gratitude. Give thanks.

- Make yourself a priority. No apologies.

- Nourish your roots.

- Faith is the willingness to receive. Have faith.

- Perfectionism is the enemy of creativity and of life. Be real, not ideal.

- Live freely.

Creative Juice

Putting It Together: Finding Your Process

We are a species of storytellers. Since firelight danced on the sides of cave homes, we have gathered to hear and learn from tales. In every culture throughout time we have "talked story"—creation stories, morality tales, bedtime stories, epic love stories, heroes' journeys, battle sagas. When we gossip, we "tell stories." Stories that are real, stories that are true but not real. Stories.

Get Juicy

Take the following situations and tell a story about each. If you get stuck, ask what each character wants, what obstacles stop them (internal and external), and what happens that changes them.

- A young nurse is strangely attracted to a ninety-year-old patient. They meet by "accident" late at night in the hospital courtyard.

- A claustrophobic man and a woman desperate for a date—strangers to each other—are trapped in a small, enclosed bus stop when a sudden storm drops a power line directly in front of them.

- An insecure boy pretends to be a "gangstah" to impress a girl he meets at an ice-cream shop. She is an alien insect life form, disguised as a Pentecostal missionary, who lusts after his armpit, a source of food on her planet—oh, all right, skip this one.

- A grocer drops a box labeled tomato soup in front of an old, well-liked customer. From the box, a baggie explodes in a cloud of suspicious white powder.

- A boy. A girl. A dance. A knife.

By now, many of you are dashing off your first book, but wait . . . there's more!! With the amazing Blendoword™, you'll slice and dice and make radish roses like the pros!

Coming From Inside a Character

Pull out some of the characters you played with in Chapter Six or make up some new ones and have them interact in the following exercise. Don't worry about dialogue for now, I'll provide it. But you'll create the characters, the setting and the nonverbal action.

- Establish a setting

  - Where is it?

  - When is it—season, day and hour

- Establish characters with conflicting goals. Maybe you'll use some from Chapter Six, maybe you'll make some new ones.

Now, create your scene, starting with this noncommittal script called an "open scene"—open, because the words can mean anything.

Open Scene

One: Hey.

Two: Hi.

One: What's up?

Two: What do you mean?

One: You know.

Two: No, I don't.

One: Yes, you do.

Two: I don't think so.

One: Sure.

Two: Whatever.

One: Right.

Consider how different this scene would be if, for example, a mother confronts her fifteen-year-old daughter over the breakfast table after the daughter has stayed out all night at a rave. The girl has always been a church-going honor student. Or, two strangers are at a deserted subway station. Person One believes Person Two is a serial killer, while Person Two thinks Person One is a beloved, long-lost best friend.

Using the open scene, establish the situation and write the subtext—the emotions underlying each line, what each one is thinking underneath the words.

Now write the scene, creating your own dialogue. What would these characters say, if you gave them the chance?

Coming From Inside Theme

Go back to Chapter Seven and review themes that matter to you. If you've gone global, get local. Maybe you've written "adventure." Get specific. Maybe you're interested in exploring the line where adventure becomes psychic disintegration, or perhaps you want to explore how adventure revitalizes a sagging sense of self. Both are about the subject of adventure, but very differently themed. What particularly do you want to explore about that subject? That will be your theme.

Get Juicy

Pick a subject:

_____

List three themes that draw you.

1. _____

_____

2. _____

_____

3. _____

_____

Put It Together

You've played with characters; you've discovered themes. You're awash in vivid sensory detail. These are your building blocks. Let's put it together into scenes, the rooms from which your ultimate literary house will be built.

A story involves one or more characters doing something. There is a beginning, also known as an inciting incident, which sets the ball rolling and causes the chain of events to begin. Often you'll start well into the action, in which case the inciting incident occurs before we enter the story, but there is one.

There is a middle, when the action rises, spikes, falls back (phew, pant, pant, give the reader a little break), spikes further, falls back, spikes more, always spiraling up toward the climax, which is the point of no return, the high point in your story where something happens, your protagonist learns something, and is forever changed.

All that's left to do after that is tie up loose ends, also known as the *denouement*. Your story may be a quiet, talky piece of great reserve—Chekhov does Derrida—but you still need rising action to a climax if it's a story and not a treatise.

My personal opinion is that even treatises would benefit from story treatment; one of my assets as a trial attorney was I told a story for my final argument. Every scene has the same structure as a story in microcosm: a beginning, middle and end, the little story of which either illuminates character or moves the big story forward, preferably both.

Mind you, I am giving you traditional dramatic structure, the way we've done it in the Western world for a long, long time. There are other ways—avant-garde, women's wave structure, postmodern moments that trail off without resolution. You can explore all that, once you get the basics down. But as with composition, it's good to learn the traditional rules so you know when you're breaking them. (For the basic rules of composition, see Appendix A at the back of the book.)

So, how do you go about constructing a scene? You already have. Remember the "coming from character" exercise? God, I'm sneaky. Here's another version.

Get Juicy

I call this visual exercise Imaging a Story.

Pull an image from your image file. Make it one with people in it, preferably doing something.

1. Briefly characterize each person in the image, either with a shorthand word, like *Father*, *Son*, *Boss*, *Housewife*, or a more descriptive characterization like "Truman is a forty-seven-year-old actuarial with a secret life as a drag queen."

2. Describe each character's emotional state. What does each character want?

3. What just happened?

4. What's about to happen?

5. How will what's happening change these people?

6. Will anybody learn or discover anything? What?

7. Does each character get what he or she wants? Or does the knowledge change what they want?

Whoa, look at you! You just wrote the outline of a story. If it's something you're attracted to, keep working with it. Show us what happened in scenes.

Finding Your Process: Theme or Character-Driven

In the "I want" exercise, you listed several themes that are important to you. Love, connection, freedom, whatever they are. In the character-building section, you discovered a few people populating your centers of gravity, your images and your collected voice types. Using setting details drawn from simple miracles or your image envelope, construct a scene. You'll do it two ways— character/intuitive and theme/analytic—to see which works best for you.

Many writers are character driven. They get to know their characters intimately then let them drive the story. Often, outlines are only very rough, then get revised or thrown out altogether because the characters go somewhere unexpected.

Other writers are theme driven, organizing everything else— setting, plot, characters, even point of view—around major themes. Still others are plot driven, and create characters that will fit their predetermined mold. The difference between character, and plot or theme driven is the difference between an organic, intuitive process versus an analytic, left-brained one.

Know your strength and play to it. In my completely undocumented experience, kinesthetics appear to be more character driven, while auditory learners seem more prone to theme/plot analysis. Visuals split in their tendencies. If you already know you tend to be more left- than right-brained, or vice-versa, you're well on your way to discovering your process.

When I entered law school, I was way more right-brained intuitive in how I thought. Perhaps it goes without saying, my first term of law school kicked me in the butt. I spent my first year learning a new language: logic. I'm glad, because now I can intentionally switch back and forth. Interestingly, though, as a practicing attorney, when I over-rode my intuition with my analytic mind, I was invariably wrong. Our native tongue knows best.

I heard *Snow Falling on Cedars* author David Gutterson speak about his process at the Florida Suncoast Writers Conference. He's exceptionally analytical and completely theme-driven, outlining everything else to illustrate his theme. Connie May Fowler, on the other hand, is a strong intuitive who follows the sometimes circuitous path her characters take her without benefit of an outline. They're both excellent writers and they're both right. Find out what works best for you.

Get Juicy

Choose a theme from your "I want" list and outline a short story or short short (less than a thousand words) illustrating it. Choose setting, plot and character specifically to amplify your message. You might want to use a scenario outline, similar to this one outlining a proposed short story.

1. **Subject/Theme.** What is the broad subject? Let's say, in my case, it's "justice." What is the particular theme? I'll choose the thin line between social activism and vigilantism.

2. **Conflict.** What is the basic conflict that illustrates the theme? In my example, a father learns the man he knows raped his eleven-year-old daughter will not be prosecuted.

3. **Characters.** What characters are needed? The father, a decent, caring man frustrated with an uncaring justice system; an overworked deputy D.A.; the daughter, deeply damaged by the attack; and the alleged rapist, a convicted child molester who is crude and bullying.

4. **Point of View.** Determine Point of View. Point of View is from whose perspective the story is told. First person, "I" —the most intimate POV; subjective third person, a particular "he" or "she"— still close, but creating more psychic distance for the reader; and third person omniscient—a tough POV and not generally tackled by any but veteran writers. If you're in a first person POV or a subjective third person POV that's really just one person's story, you can only write what that person would experience and think. Even with omniscient third person, change POV sparingly no more than once per scene. New writers often bounce from head to head— very distracting to a reader. I choose subjective third person from the father's POV.

5. **Setting.** Where and when is the story set? How does the setting contribute to and illustrate the theme? I choose a contemporary, middle-class neighborhood in a large, callous city. So, I wouldn't choose Chicago, a composite of neighborhoods, but might choose L.A. where car-dependence militates against knowing one's neighbors.

6. **Genre.** What style is best for my theme and plot? Realism? Comedy? And if so, what type—slapstick, farce, satire, parody, wit? Horror/gothic? Mystery? Melodrama (emotionally bigger-than-life realism—think soap operas)? Science fiction? Romance? I'm thinking a serious realistic tone best suits my story.

7. **Basic Storyline.** My story opens in the D.A.'s office, where a deputy informs the father that his daughter's rapist will not be prosecuted for lack of evidence, even though the

defendant is a known child molester who has trailed the daughter on numerous occasions.

Enraged and desperate—his daughter has been severely emotionally damaged by the attack—the father sets out to ruin the suspect, using his knowledge of computers to financially and socially bankrupt the man. With each escalating action, the father taunts him. There is nothing the suspect can do, nowhere he can go to be free. Finally he breaks and commits suicide. Shortly after, the deputy D.A. calls the father to tell him the actual rapist has confessed.

Fill out a scenario for your story. Then write it. Typically, your scenes will be of germinal actions, telling moments that make the story. Not always, but usually.

Get Juicy

Choose two characters from the Building Character Down to the Ground chapter or cast completely new characters. Then let the characters tell their story. What does each character want more than anything? How does the other character stand in the way? How does the protagonist overcome obstacles, both external obstacles like a thwarting character, and internal obstacles like self-doubt? Let the character do the work; you write it down. I like to lie on the couch during this stage, close my eyes and watch. You may want to start with two characters who have conflicting goals and see where they lead.

If you loved the analytic-outline method and thought the character-driven story was flakier than crust, you're a deductive, left-brain thinker. If, on the other foot, you loved watching your character tell her story but would rather have crawled across cut glass than outline a story based on theme, you're a strong intuitive, right-brainer.

One method will probably emerge as far more natural to you than the other, although you may be one of the fortunate people who think as well from either side of the brain. If you found both exercises equally accessible, sell your clothes—you've gone to heaven. You're an ambicognitive shape-shifter who is fluent in both right and left hemispheres.

The Importance of Community

Creating is an isolated activity. It's just you and a glowing screen in a darkened room. Or you and a canvas. You and a piano. Maybe that's why I've been drawn to the performing arts—they allow me to express myself creatively without sacrificing community. As I lean into my older years though, I find quieter arts more appealing. But still lonely.

Make a point of establishing a community of like-minded creative types. Join or start a writers' group. Check out your local university or a large bookstore or library. Libraries, by the way, will often let writers' groups meet for free. Voilà. Instant locale.

Writers' conferences are great places to network and perhaps form continuing support groups. Writing classes offer probably the best chance of finding and keeping your tribe. However you do it, do it! Aside from the very practical free editing and publishing advice you'll receive from a peer group, the strength of having caring people at your back can't be overestimated. A writers' group is your oak when the winds come. The continuing belief in your work when your own belief wavers.

Get Juicy

Gather your writers' group or a group of friends and have a "Sound Party." Sit in a circle, knees touching. Instruct the group to consider the following types of sounds: "white" sounds like buzzes and hisses and hums; percussive sounds like pops and clicks and snaps and claps; elongated vowel sounds—aaaay, eeeee, aaaah, oooooh, ooooo; harmonic sounds.

Choose a theme, for example, "Birth of the Universe," or perhaps "A Day at the Circus," or maybe "The Restless Jungle." Or make up your own title. Just be sure it involves a lot of potential sound. Close your eyes. Now, create a sound picture. You can trust there will be a beginning, middle and end. You can also trust that the process will create something wonderful. When you're done, take out journals and write about it.

As long as you've got them together, try some Human Music. Stand in a circle, arms around each other so each participant can feel the next person's breathing. Instruct the group to consider the same types of sounds you used for the "Sound Party": "white" sounds like buzzes and hisses and hums; percussive sounds like pops and clicks and snaps and claps; elongated vowel sounds—aaaay, eeeee, aaaah, oooooh, ooooo; harmonic sounds. With no predetermined theme, close your eyes and see what happens. When the last sound fades, open your eyes and look around. Simple miracles. Write about it.

For the visual-kinesthetics, have a Calder mobile party, where words form on the edge of balance. Instructions are in Appendix B at the back of this book.

Peer Critique

One of the greatest blessings of a writing community is the peer critique of your work it affords. There's only one proper response to criticism offered in good faith: "Thank you." Set aside defensiveness, explanations, saucy retorts. Say thank you, note the comment and see if it applies. Others are able to hear clunkers when you can't from being too close to the work. Some comments are totally off the wall. Some are gold that when mined will make your work glow.

If you don't have a writers' group to assist you with objective evaluation, or even if you do, try these two similar tools. First, read your work out loud. Always. You'll hear what you couldn't see—hidden ambushes, inadvertent redundancies and homonyms, ill-fitting syntax. Second, put your writing in a drawer and don't go back to it until you can observe it with fresh—preferably disinterested—eyes. Read it out loud again. You'll be astounded. And well on your way to a good rewrite.

Critique with grace. Always give a rose before a thorn, a compliment before a suggestion on how to improve the writing. Be specific. "I didn't like it" helps nobody. Ditto, "I liked it." What specifically did you like or not like? Is the work cluttered with too many adverbs and adjectives? Run-on sentences that leave the reader in the dust? Insufficiently detailed characterizations? Point of View problems?

Critique with the same mindset you have when receiving: as the gifts they are.

Sybil's Story

I leave you with one of my favorite stories, the myth of Sybil. I've heard this told in different ways; I offer the one that moved me most deeply.

> Sybil was a wild, creative woman who lived in ancient times. She created heart and soul, speaking her truth always, unfettered by social convention. This made her a very dangerous woman and the authorities were determined to stop her before she contaminated the rest of the subdued populace. They passed laws forbidding Sybil from creating her art works. She changed to a different medium. More laws were passed. Sybil would not be stopped.
>
> The powers that be personally met with Sybil and sought to stifle her with their most intimidating methods. Sybil would not be stopped.
>
> Finally, the authorities stripped Sybil of everything—all her art tools, all her pens, all her paper. They stripped her of her very garments and threw her into a cave with nothing.
>
> On the floor of the cave, Sybil found dried leaves. Using her own blood, Sybil wrote her truth on the leaves. Sybil would not be stopped.

* * *

My wish for you is that you not be stopped. That you speak your truth in love, creatively and fully, for all your days.

Appendix A: The Rules

Like all rules, these may be broken at times to good effect, but know them before you break them and choose accordingly.

1. Verbs have to agree with their subjects.

2. Don't end sentences with prepositions.

3. Avoid starting sentences with conjunctions such as "and," "or," or "but."

4. The infinitive should stay together, e.g., "It's wrong normally to split an infinitive," not "It's wrong to normally split an infinitive."

5. Find a fresh way to say hackneyed phrases such as "like the plague," or "old hat."

6. Avoid using words beginning with the same letter several times in a row. Posturing palpably proliferates, presumably.

7. Use the specific rather the general. "God lies in the details." Make it a Ferrari instead of just a sports car.

8. Avoid parentheses; use commas or dashes instead.

9. Avoid the Department of Redundancy Department. Once is enough! Don't beat the reader over the head with it. Oh, wait, did I just say that?

10. Use complete sentences with a subject, a verb and an object. Don't put together two complete clauses with only a comma; use a semicolon or separate them into two sentences. Sentence fragments are as bad as comma splices and run-ons.

11. Write out contractions—"are not" instead of "aren't"—when writing formally. However, in fiction or when using a conversational tone contractions are fine.

12. Stick with words your reading audience knows. Rather than "cogitate the viscissitudes," wouldn't you rather simply "think about the changes"?

13. Broad overstatements aren't as helpful as specific ideas.

14. Don't use double negatives.

15. Write out "and" and abbreviations rather than using "&" or, for example, "etc."

16. Normally, sentences need at least a subject, a verb and an object.

17. Use the active rather than the passive voice. Avoid using verb forms of "to be." Write, "He hit the ball," rather than "He was hitting the ball."

18. Eliminate commas that are not necessary. Parenthetical words, however, should be enclosed in commas.

19. Don't use a big word when a small one will do. Use the most appropriate word, not the one that best shows off your vocabulary.

20. Use exclamation points very sparingly.

21. Use words correctly, regardless of how others use them; for example, "irregardless" is not a word.

22. Use the apostrophe in its proper place and omit it when not needed. Ask if it would work without the apostrophe by adding "is," for example, "it's" becomes "it is." If not, e.g., "its leaves were green," then don't use the apostrophe. Hers, yours, and ours NEVER take an apostrophe.

23. Except in fiction, quotes should be used sparingly and, for both fiction and nonfiction, should advance the story with new information, not simply affirm something already stated.

24. Resist hyperbole. Overstating your case decreases credibility. At the same time, don't understate earth-shattering ideas.

25. Avoid regional colloquialisms, except in fiction or when intentionally introduced to provide local color. That dog won't hunt.

26. Don't mix metaphors.

27. Avoid rhetorical questions.If you don't actually expect an answer—the definition of a rhetorical question—then say it as a statement. Too many questions can be annoying.

28. Avoid exaggeration.

29. Proofread carefully. This speaks itself.

Appendix B: Calder Mobiles

Have each artist write his or her truths on shapes of heavy cardboard or, if you really want to get fancy, etch copper leaves with a jeweler's engraving tool. (I've never done this, but always wanted to.) If you use cardboard, duplicate the exact shapes used in lighter weight paper. These will be glued together over florist wire.

A mobile is essentially a set of tiers that teeter like scales. You need to find the fulcrum point of each part, then attach it there to the next part.

1. Start with a rough drawing. Do you want your mobile to spread or droop? An alternative plan for those of us who jump in and see what happens is to start and organically let it unfold. Take the emotional temperature of the group. You may want to make two distinct, but interrelated structures, a left-brain pre-planned and a right-brain serendipitous.

2. Gather materials:

   • Heavy cardboard cut in different shapes, found objects—anything you can write on. Surprisingly, flat is better than 3-D shapes; 3-D tends to look the same from every angle, while flat shapes change – circles become lines which become half circles, which become lines.

   • Scissors and Exacto knives

   • A hook to hang the mobile from as you're making it

   • 12 to 18 gauge wire to make cross beams. Skip coat hangers—too rigid. Make the wire galvanized, especially if you plan on hanging it outside. Craft shops should have this.

- Something to hang the pieces with—glue, wire, s-hooks. I find the little hangers used with fishing lures to be the best for lightweight objects.

3. Once your materials are gathered, cut out the individual objects. If you're using cardboard, use Exacto knives or scissors, depending on thickness. Be sure each individual piece pleases your eye. Rarely will a bunch of unpleasing individual objects coalesce into an aesthetic whole.

    One easy method you might try is cardboard on the bottom, heavy paper cut to the exact shape as the cardboard on the top.

    Make s-hooks using 28-gauge wire, needle-nose pliers and a nail or pencil to wrap the wire around. Do NOT cut your cross beams in advance. Those will need to be tinkered with as you go.

4. Assemble! Here's what Calder said about assembling: "You put a disc here (at one end of the cross-beam) and then you put a triangle at the other end and then you balance them on your finger and keep adding . . . I begin with the smallest [shape] and work up. Once I know the balance point for the first pair of discs, I anchor it by a hook and so on up. It's a kind of ascending scale of weights and counter-weights." Note: Calder built from the bottom up for a reason; it's the easiest way to go.

    Start with two shapes on the bottom tier. Link them with wire, allowing extra inches at each end for a graceful curve and for attachment. Attach.

    Next, find the balance point: hold out your index finger as a fulcrum and set the tier across it. Slide the crossbeam along with your other hand until it rests at the angle you want. Make a loop (to which you'll attach your second tier) where the wire rests on your finger. Loops should face up, not down and be as round as can be so they'll twirl better. You can make your loops with needle-nosed pliers or by bending around a pencil. Bend <u>against</u> the curve, not with.

Repeat as needed. Find your balance and create. Together.

After you've finished, have the group sit down and write personal essays entitled "Balance." Share what you've written.